ASVAB NAVY
Practice Test Book

A Comprehensive ASVAB Study Guide to Ace the Exam with over 500 Practice Questions, Detailed Answers, Insightful Rationale, and Exam Strategies for Success

Dale B. Cobos

Copyright © 2023 Dale B. Cobos - All rights reserved.

No part of this publication may be reproduced, stored in a retrieval system, or transmitted in any form or by any means, electronic, mechanical, photocopying, recording, and scanning without permission in writing by the author

Contents

Chapter 1

Introduction 1

  Understanding The ASVAB 2

  Importance of the ASVAB for Navy Recruits 5

  Structure of the ASVAB 8

  Scoring System of the ASVAB 11

Chapter 2

General Science 15

  Overview and Study Guide 15

  Practice Test with Answers 19

  General Science Test Strategies 46

Chapter 3

Arithmetic Reasoning 50

  Overview and Study Guide 50

  Practice Test with Answers 55

  Arithmetic Reasoning Test Strategies 79

Chapter 4

Word Knowledge **83**

    Overview and Study Guide 83

    Word Knowledge Practice Test with Answers 85

    Word Knowledge Test Strategies 107

Chapter 5

Paragraph Comprehension **111**

    Overview and Study Guide 111

    Practice Test with Answers 113

    Paragraph Comprehension Test Strategies 154

Chapter 6

Mathematics Knowledge **157**

    Overview and Study Guide 157

    Practice Test with Answers 159

    Mathematics Knowledge Test Strategies 178

Chapter 7

Electronics Information **181**

    Overview and Study Guide 181

Practice Test with Answers 183

Test Strategies.. 205

Chapter 8

Auto and Shop Information...208

Overview and Study Guide 208

Practice Test with Answers 211

Test Strategies.. 235

Chapter 9

Mechanical Comprehension..239

Overview and Study Guide 239

Practice Test with Answers 242

Test Strategies.. 264

Chapter 10

Assembling Objects..268

Overview and Study Guide 268

Practice Test with Answers 270

Test Strategies.. 281

Chapter 11

Exam Day Tips and Strategies..**284**

  Preparing for the Test Day 284

  Strategies for During the Test...................................... 286

  What to Do After the Test 289

Chapter 12

Conclusion **292**

  Key Takeaways 294

  Further Study Recommendations................................. 296

Chapter 1

Introduction

Welcome to your comprehensive guide to the Armed Services Vocational Aptitude Battery (ASVAB) for Navy recruits. This guide is designed to equip you with the necessary tools, skills, and knowledge required to excel in the ASVAB exam and secure a place in the U.S Navy.

The ASVAB is a multiple-choice test, administered by the United States Military Entrance Processing Command, utilized to determine qualification for enlistment in the United States Armed Forces. It is crucial not just for the purposes of enlistment, but it also helps the military understand the prospective recruit's strengths and potential future job placements within the Navy.

This guidebook is structured to cover all sections of the ASVAB, which include General Science, Arithmetic Reasoning, Word Knowledge, Paragraph Comprehension, Mathematics Knowledge, Electronics

Information, Auto and Shop Information, Mechanical Comprehension, and Assembling Objects. Each chapter will provide an in-depth overview of the section, a study guide that breaks down the concepts in easy, understandable language, a set of unique practice questions, and proven strategies to handle that section of the test.

Understanding The ASVAB

The Armed Services Vocational Aptitude Battery, or ASVAB, is a series of tests that determine the qualifications of an individual for enlistment in the United States military. Although it is most commonly associated with the U.S. Army, the ASVAB is not exclusive to it; it is also used by the Navy, Marine Corps, Air Force, Coast Guard, and the Space Force.

ASVAB serves two main purposes. First, it determines whether you are eligible to join the military service. Each branch of the military has its own minimum score requirement. Secondly, it helps to identify which Military Occupational Specialties (MOS) you might be best suited for. In simpler terms, the test helps the military to place you in a job where your skills and abilities can be utilized to their fullest extent.

The ASVAB test is divided into multiple sections, each designed to measure your knowledge and skills in a specific area. Here are the sections that you'll find on the ASVAB:

1. **General Science (GS):** This section measures your knowledge of basic science principles.

2. **Arithmetic Reasoning (AR):** This section gauges your ability to solve basic arithmetic problems.

3. **Word Knowledge (WK):** This section measures your understanding and knowledge of words and their meanings.

4. **Paragraph Comprehension (PC):** This section tests your ability to understand and interpret written material.

5. **Mathematics Knowledge (MK):** This section measures your knowledge of basic mathematical concepts and applications.

6. **Electronics Information (EI):** This section gauges your knowledge of electrical equipment

and parts, including currents, circuits, devices, and systems.

7. **Auto and Shop Information (AS):** This section measures your knowledge of automotive maintenance and repair, as well as wood and metal shop practices.

8. **Mechanical Comprehension (MC):** This section gauges your understanding of basic mechanical and physical principles.

9. **Assembling Objects (AO):** This section tests your ability to determine how an object will look when its parts are put together.

The first four sections—General Science, Arithmetic Reasoning, Word Knowledge, and Paragraph Comprehension—make up the Armed Forces Qualification Test (AFQT) score. This score is used to determine your eligibility for enlistment in the military. The remaining sections help determine your job placement within the military.

Preparing for the ASVAB involves studying and understanding the different types of questions you might encounter in each section. A higher score increases your chances of not only joining the military but also landing a job that aligns with your skills and interests.

This book, "ASVAB Navy Practice Test," is designed to be your companion as you embark on this journey. Through comprehensive overviews, practical strategies, and practice tests, it aims to make your ASVAB preparation effective and manageable. In the chapters ahead, we'll dive deeper into each section, providing guidance and practice to help you ace the test. Remember, your effort and determination will play crucial roles in your success. Good luck!

Importance of the ASVAB for Navy Recruits

Joining the U.S. Navy is a significant decision, and one of the critical steps in that process is taking the Armed Services Vocational Aptitude Battery, or ASVAB. The importance of this test for Navy recruits cannot be overstated, and here's why.

The ASVAB is more than just a test that determines your eligibility to join the military service; it's an instrumental tool that aids in shaping your military career.

Determining Eligibility for Enlistment:

First and foremost, the ASVAB is used to determine your eligibility for enlistment in the Navy. To qualify for enlistment, you must achieve a minimum score on the ASVAB. This score, known as the Armed Forces Qualification Test (AFQT) score, is derived from four sections of the ASVAB: General Science, Arithmetic Reasoning, Word Knowledge, and Paragraph Comprehension.

In the U.S. Navy, at the time of writing, the minimum AFQT score needed for enlistment is 35, though waivers may be available in some cases for scores as low as 31. However, keep in mind that these are just the minimum requirements, and a higher score will make you more competitive among other recruits.

Identifying Suitable Job Roles:

In addition to determining your eligibility, the ASVAB plays a critical role in identifying which jobs or roles, known as ratings in the Navy, you are most qualified for. Your scores in all the sections of the ASVAB are used to create composite scores, which the Navy uses to determine which ratings you're most suited for.

For instance, if you score highly on the Electronics Information section of the ASVAB, you might be an excellent candidate for a rating like Electronics Technician. A high score in the Mechanical Comprehension section might indicate that you're well-suited for a rating like Machinist's Mate.

Therefore, it's important to note that every section of the ASVAB matters when it comes to determining your job placement, even those not included in the AFQT score. Excelling in a wide range of sections can open more doors and provide more options when it comes to your career in the Navy.

Impacting Your Navy Career:

Finally, your ASVAB scores can have a lasting impact on your Navy career. Ratings not only determine your day-to-day duties in the Navy but also impact your opportunities for advancement and even your post-military career. High ASVAB scores can lead to more desirable ratings with better promotion potential and more advanced training opportunities. These, in turn, can translate into valuable skills and experience for the civilian job market once your time in the Navy is over.

In conclusion, the ASVAB is an essential step on your path to becoming a Navy recruit. Not only does it establish your eligibility to serve, but it also provides the Navy with a clear idea of where your talents lie, ensuring that you can serve in a capacity that benefits both you and the Navy. Your ASVAB score is more than just a number; it's the starting point of your military career. So, take the time to prepare for it well—it's an investment in your future.

Structure of the ASVAB

Now that we've understood the importance of the ASVAB, let's dive deeper into its structure. The ASVAB is designed to evaluate your abilities and knowledge across a broad array of subjects. It consists of ten subtests, each focusing on a different area. Here are those subtests:

1. **General Science (GS):** This section is a measure of your knowledge in life science, earth science, and physical science. You'll face a range of

questions covering various topics such as biology, chemistry, environmental science, and more.

2. **Arithmetic Reasoning (AR):** Here, your ability to solve arithmetic word problems is tested. You'll be asked to analyze problems and determine the necessary steps to find the solution.

3. **Word Knowledge (WK):** This part of the ASVAB measures your understanding of word meanings through synonyms. It tests your vocabulary and ability to determine the meaning of words in context.

4. **Paragraph Comprehension (PC):** This section requires you to read passages and understand the content to answer related questions. It tests your ability to interpret written information.

5. **Mathematics Knowledge (MK):** This subtest measures your understanding of high school level mathematical principles. It includes topics like algebra, geometry, and basic trigonometry.

6. **Electronics Information (EI):** This section tests your knowledge of basic electronic principles and

terminologies. Topics include electrical currents, circuits, devices, and electronic systems.

7. **Auto and Shop Information (AS):** This part of the ASVAB measures your understanding of automobile technology and basic shop terminology and practices. It tests knowledge related to car maintenance, repair, and woodworking.

8. **Mechanical Comprehension (MC):** This section evaluates your understanding of mechanical principles and mechanisms. It covers topics such as the laws of physics, identifying tools, and simple machines.

9. **Assembling Objects (AO):** This subtest measures your spatial visualization ability and understanding of how mechanical parts fit together. You'll be asked to choose the correct image of an object after it's assembled.

10. **Verbal Expression (VE):** Although this is not a separate subtest, the Verbal Expression score is derived from the Word Knowledge and Paragraph Comprehension sections, and it's a part of the AFQT score calculation.

Each of these subtests has a different number of questions and time limits. Together, they provide a comprehensive overview of your academic ability and vocational aptitude, which are vital for your future role in the Navy.

Understanding the structure of the ASVAB is the first step in effective test preparation. Knowing what to expect will help you allocate your study time wisely, focusing on the areas that need the most improvement.

In the following chapters of this book, we'll provide an in-depth look at each section of the ASVAB, including subject overviews, study guides, practice questions, and test-taking strategies. It's important to remember that preparation is key to achieving a high ASVAB score and ultimately pursuing a fulfilling career in the U.S. Navy. Let's set sail on your journey to success!

Scoring System of the ASVAB

Understanding the scoring system of the ASVAB is just as crucial as understanding the content of the test. This system can seem a little complex at first, but let's break it down to make it easier to understand.

There are two types of scores that you'll receive from the ASVAB: the Standard Scores and the Composite or Line Scores.

Standard Scores:

Every subtest in the ASVAB is scored separately on a scale of 1 to 100. These are your Standard Scores. They represent how your performance on a subtest matches up with that of the general population. The mean, or average score, is set to 50.

This means if you scored 60 on a subtest, you performed better than 60% of the general population who took the test. A standard score of 50 indicates you scored right in the middle of the general population.

Armed Forces Qualification Test (AFQT) Score:

From these Standard Scores, the AFQT score is derived. This score is the one that's used to determine whether you're eligible to enlist in the military. It's calculated from four subtests: Arithmetic Reasoning (AR), Mathematics Knowledge (MK), Word Knowledge (WK), and Paragraph Comprehension (PC).

Your raw scores from these sections are converted into your AFQT score, which is then presented as a percentile between 1 and 99. This percentile score reflects what percentage of the test-taking population you scored higher than. For example, an AFQT score of 65 means you scored better than 65% of all test-takers.

Remember, each branch of the military has its own minimum AFQT score requirements for enlistment. As of the writing of this book, the minimum AFQT score for enlistment in the Navy is 35, but higher scores will make you more competitive among other recruits.

Composite or Line Scores:

In addition to your Standard and AFQT scores, you'll receive what's called Composite or Line Scores. These are combinations of your standard scores from the various subtests and are used to determine your qualification for specific job roles or ratings in the Navy.

Each branch of the military uses its own formula to calculate these composite scores. For instance, a specific job in the Navy may require a certain score on a composite calculated from your performance in the Arithmetic Reasoning, Mathematics Knowledge, and Mechanical Comprehension sections.

In the following chapters, we'll explore each subtest in detail, guiding you through the kind of questions you can expect and providing strategies to help you score well. By fully understanding the structure and scoring of the ASVAB, you can effectively strategize your preparation and give yourself the best shot at a high score and a fulfilling career in the U.S. Navy. Stay the course; your journey is just beginning!

Chapter 2
General Science

Overview and Study Guide

The General Science (GS) section of the ASVAB assesses your knowledge and comprehension of various areas of science. This section serves as an indicator of your ability to understand, remember, and apply scientific principles and concepts.

Overview

The General Science section is a mix of questions from life science, physical science, and earth and space science. Let's delve into what each of these domains entail:

1. **Life Science:** This includes topics like basic biology, human health, and living organisms. You might encounter questions about cellular function, human anatomy, or the principles of genetics.

2. **Physical Science:** Here, you'll find questions that deal with physics and chemistry. Expect to be

tested on topics like basic principles of motion, energy, light, sound, and basic concepts of atomic structure and chemical reactions.

3. **Earth and Space Science:** This part covers topics related to geology, meteorology, and astronomy. You might see questions about rock formations, weather patterns, and the solar system.

Study Guide

The General Science section can feel overwhelming due to its broad scope. However, with the right study approach, you can be well-prepared for this section. Here are some tips and strategies to help you study for the General Science subtest:

1. **Identify Your Weaknesses:** Take a few practice tests to identify which areas of general science you need to work on the most. Spend more time reviewing these areas.

2. **Create a Study Plan:** Allocate your study time effectively. Don't try to cover all topics in one session. Break down your study periods into manageable chunks focusing on one topic at a time.

3. **Use Reliable Study Materials:** Use textbooks, online resources, and this guide to review and understand science concepts. Watch educational videos to help visualize difficult concepts.

4. **Make Flashcards:** Flashcards are a great way to memorize facts and details. You can make them for different categories, such as 'life science', 'physical science', and 'earth and space science', and review them regularly.

5. **Understand, Don't Just Memorize:** While memorization might help with some facts, it's more important to understand the concepts and principles in science. This will allow you to apply your knowledge to different types of questions.

6. **Practice Regularly:** Regular practice is key to doing well on the test. Regularly take practice tests to familiarize yourself with the question format and improve your speed and accuracy.

Here are some sample topics you may want to review for each science category:

Life Science:

- Basic Biology: Cell structure, DNA, and genetics

- Human Anatomy: Systems of the body (digestive, respiratory, circulatory, etc.)
- Ecology: Food chains, ecosystems, and environmental science

Physical Science:

- Physics: Laws of motion, energy, and basic principles of electricity
- Chemistry: Atomic structure, states of matter, and basic chemical reactions

Earth and Space Science:

- Geology: Types of rocks, the structure of Earth
- Meteorology: Weather patterns, atmospheric layers
- Astronomy: Basic facts about the solar system, stars, and galaxies

The General Science section is your chance to demonstrate your understanding of the natural world. With the right preparation, you can turn this broad section into a strong asset on the ASVAB. Use the strategies in this chapter to prepare efficiently and effectively. Happy studying!

Practice Test with Answers

In this part of the chapter, we will provide a selection of sample questions, with answers and explanations, to help you prepare for the General Science section of the ASVAB.

1. **Question:** Which of the following best describes the function of white blood cells?

- A) They carry oxygen from the lungs to the rest of the body.
- B) They are involved in clotting blood.
- C) They fight off infections and diseases.
- D) They provide energy to the body.

Answer: C) They fight off infections and diseases.

Explanation: White blood cells, or leukocytes, play an essential role in the body's immune system. They help the body fight off infections and diseases by attacking harmful bacteria, viruses, and other foreign invaders.

2. **Question:** Which of the following is the primary gas in Earth's atmosphere?

- A) Oxygen
- B) Hydrogen

- C) Nitrogen
- D) Carbon Dioxide

Answer: C) Nitrogen

Explanation: Nitrogen makes up about 78% of the Earth's atmosphere, making it the most abundant gas. Oxygen is the second most abundant gas, making up about 21% of the atmosphere.

3. **Question:** In the water cycle, what is the process of water vapor turning into liquid water?
- A) Evaporation
- B) Condensation
- C) Precipitation
- D) Transpiration

Answer: B) Condensation

Explanation: In the water cycle, condensation is the process where water vapor in the air cools down and turns back into liquid water. This often forms clouds in the Earth's atmosphere.

4. **Question:** In a basic chemical reaction, what are the substances that result from the reaction called?
- A) Reactants

- B) Products
- C) Compounds
- D) Elements

   Answer: B) Products

   Explanation: In a chemical reaction, the substances that you start with, called reactants, interact to form new substances, called products.

5. **Question:** What type of rock is formed from the cooling and solidifying of magma or lava?
- A) Metamorphic
- B) Sedimentary
- C) Igneous
- D) Limestone

   Answer: C) Igneous

   Explanation: Igneous rocks are formed from the cooling and solidification of magma (from inside the Earth) or lava (magma that has reached the Earth's surface).

6. **Question:** Which planet is known as the "Red Planet"?
- A) Mars

- B) Jupiter
- C) Saturn
- D) Venus

   Answer: A) Mars

   Explanation: Mars is often referred to as the "Red Planet" because of its reddish appearance, caused by iron oxide (rust) on its surface.

7. **Question:** What part of the cell contains the genetic material?
- A) Nucleus
- B) Mitochondria
- C) Cytoplasm
- D) Cell wall

   Answer: A) Nucleus

   Explanation: The nucleus is the control center of the cell and contains the cell's genetic material (DNA).

8. **Question:** Which law of motion states that an object at rest stays at rest and an object in motion stays in motion with the same speed and in the

same direction unless acted upon by an unbalanced force?

- A) Newton's First Law
- B) Newton's Second Law
- C) Newton's Third Law
- D) Newton's Fourth Law

Answer: A) Newton's First Law

Explanation: This statement is Newton's First Law, also known as the law of inertia. It describes the motion of an object when no force is applied.

9. **Question:** What is the process of plants using sunlight to synthesize foods with the help of chlorophyll?

- A) Respiration
- B) Digestion
- C) Photosynthesis
- D) Fermentation

Answer: C) Photosynthesis

Explanation: Photosynthesis is the process by which green plants, algae, and some bacteria use sunlight, carbon dioxide, and water to produce glucose (food) and oxygen, with the help of chlorophyll.

10. **Question:** What phase change occurs when a solid turns directly into a gas?

- A) Evaporation
- B) Melting
- C) Sublimation
- D) Freezing

Answer: C) Sublimation

Explanation: Sublimation is the phase change in which a substance changes directly from a solid to a gas, without passing through the liquid phase. An example of sublimation in everyday life is dry ice (solid carbon dioxide), which sublimates at room temperature and pressure.

11. **Question:** What type of organism makes its own food using light or chemical energy?

- A) Herbivore
- B) Carnivore
- C) Autotroph
- D) Heterotroph

Answer: C) Autotroph

Explanation: Autotrophs, such as plants and certain types of bacteria, can make their own food through photosynthesis (using light energy) or chemosynthesis (using chemical energy).

12. **Question:** Which of the following is NOT a type of simple machine?

- A) Lever
- B) Pulley
- C) Bicycle
- D) Wheel and Axle

Answer: C) Bicycle

Explanation: A bicycle is not a simple machine. It is a complex machine made up of several simple machines. The other options - lever, pulley, and wheel and axle - are all types of simple machines.

13. **Question:** What is the densest layer of the Earth?

- A) Crust
- B) Mantle
- C) Outer Core

- D) Inner Core

    Answer: D) Inner Core

Explanation: The inner core, composed mostly of iron and nickel, is the densest layer of the Earth. It is also the hottest layer, with temperatures similar to the surface of the Sun.

14. **Question:** In the periodic table, elements in the same vertical column are most similar in terms of what?

- A) Atomic mass
- B) Number of protons
- C) Chemical properties
- D) Physical state

    Answer: C) Chemical properties

Explanation: In the periodic table, elements in the same vertical column, or group, have similar chemical properties. This is because they have the same number of valence electrons, which largely determine an element's chemical behavior.

15. **Question:** Which of the following is a measure of the amount of matter an object has?

- A) Volume
- B) Mass
- C) Density
- D) Weight

Answer: B) Mass

Explanation: Mass is a measure of the amount of matter in an object. Unlike weight, it is not dependent on gravity and remains the same no matter where the object is in the universe.

16. **Question:** What is the atomic number of an atom?
    - A) The number of neutrons in the nucleus
    - B) The number of protons in the nucleus
    - C) The sum of protons and neutrons in the nucleus
    - D) The sum of protons and electrons in the atom

    Answer: B) The number of protons in the nucleus

    Explanation: The atomic number of an atom is equal to the number of protons in its nucleus. This number defines the identity of an element.

17. **Question:** In the human body, which system is responsible for the breakdown of food into nutrients?

- A) Circulatory system
- B) Nervous system
- C) Respiratory system
- D) Digestive system

Answer: D) Digestive system

Explanation: The digestive system is responsible for breaking down food into nutrients that the body can use for energy, growth, and cell repair.

18. **Question:** Which planet in our solar system is known for its beautiful ring system?

- A) Jupiter
- B) Venus
- C) Saturn
- D) Mars

Answer: C) Saturn

Explanation: Saturn is known for its extensive and bright ring system, which is made of ice particles with a smaller amount of rocky debris and dust.

19. **Question:** What is the primary function of the respiratory system?

- A) To transport oxygen and nutrients to the body's cells
- B) To filter waste products from the blood
- C) To protect the body from diseases
- D) To absorb oxygen and expel carbon dioxide

    Answer: D) To absorb oxygen and expel carbon dioxide

Explanation: The primary function of the respiratory system is to absorb oxygen from the air we breathe and expel carbon dioxide, which is a waste product of cellular respiration.

20. **Question:** What kind of organism breaks down dead organic material?

- A) Producer
- B) Consumer
- C) Decomposer
- D) Herbivore

    Answer: C) Decomposer

Explanation: Decomposers, like fungi and bacteria, break down dead plants and animals into organic materials, which return to the soil and can be used by plants for growth.

21. **Question:** What is the speed of light?
- A) 186,000 miles per hour
- B) 186,000 miles per second
- C) 186,000 kilometers per hour
- D) 186,000 kilometers per second

    Answer: B) 186,000 miles per second

Explanation: The speed of light in a vacuum is approximately 186,282 miles per second.

22. **Question:** What do you call the transfer of heat through the movement of a fluid (liquid or gas)?
- A) Conduction
- B) Convection
- C) Radiation
- D) Sublimation

    Answer: B) Convection

Explanation: Convection is the transfer of heat through the movement of a fluid, such as water in a pot or air in the atmosphere.

23. **Question:** What are the building blocks of proteins?

- A) Nucleotides
- B) Fatty acids
- C) Amino acids
- D) Glucose

    Answer: C) Amino acids

Explanation: Proteins are made up of amino acids. There are 20 different types of amino acids that can be combined to make a protein.

24. **Question:** Which of these is not a component of Darwin's Theory of Evolution?

- A) Natural Selection
- B) Survival of the Fittest
- C) Genetic Drift
- D) Law of Inertia

    Answer: D) Law of Inertia

Explanation: The Law of Inertia is a principle of physics as described by Newton, not a component of Darwin's Theory of Evolution.

25. **Question:** What is a comet composed of?

- A) Iron and nickel
- B) Dust, rock, and frozen gases
- C) Lava and magma
- D) Pure ice

Answer: B) Dust, rock, and frozen gases

Explanation: Comets are composed of dust, rock, and frozen gases like water, ammonia, methane and carbon dioxide. When they come close to the Sun, the heat causes the frozen gases to vaporize, creating a visible coma or envelope around the nucleus and often a tail.

26. **Question:** What is the main purpose of DNA?

- A) To control the activities of the cell
- B) To provide energy to the cell
- C) To protect the cell from viruses
- D) To help the cell move

Answer: A) To control the activities of the cell

Explanation: The main purpose of DNA is to store information that tells the cells how to function and reproduce. It serves as the blueprint for proteins, which carry out most of the work in cells.

27. **Question:** Which force is responsible for keeping planets in orbit around the sun?

- A) Magnetic force
- B) Frictional force
- C) Gravitational force
- D) Nuclear force

   Answer: C) Gravitational force

Explanation: Gravitational force is the force of attraction between two masses. It's this force that keeps planets in their orbits around the sun.

28. **Question:** What is the primary function of the mitochondria in a cell?

- A) To control the cell's activities
- B) To produce proteins
- C) To produce energy
- D) To protect the cell from viruses

   Answer: C) To produce energy

Explanation: The primary function of the mitochondria, often called the "powerhouse of the cell," is to convert the energy stored in glucose into ATP (adenosine triphosphate), a form of energy that cells can use.

29. **Question:** What is a group of similar cells that work together to perform a specific function called?

- A) Organ
- B) Organ system
- C) Tissue
- D) Organism

Answer: C) Tissue

Explanation: A group of similar cells that work together to perform a specific function is called a tissue. Examples include muscle tissue, nervous tissue, and epithelial tissue.

30. **Question:** What type of energy is stored in an object due to its position or shape?

- A) Kinetic energy
- B) Thermal energy
- C) Potential energy

- D) Mechanical energy

    Answer: C) Potential energy

Explanation: Potential energy is the energy stored in an object due to its position (such as a book on a shelf) or shape (such as a stretched spring or a drawn bow).

31. **Question:** Which part of the human brain is primarily responsible for coordinating muscle movements and maintaining balance?

- A) Cerebrum
- B) Cerebellum
- C) Brainstem
- D) Hypothalamus

    Answer: B) Cerebellum

Explanation: The cerebellum, located at the back of the brain, is primarily responsible for coordinating voluntary muscle movements and maintaining posture, balance, and equilibrium.

32. **Question:** What type of bond involves the transfer of electrons from one atom to another?

- A) Covalent bond
- B) Ionic bond

- C) Hydrogen bond
- D) Metallic bond

    Answer: B) Ionic bond

Explanation: In an ionic bond, one atom donates one or more electrons to another atom, resulting in the formation of positive and negative ions. The ions are held together by the force of attraction between opposite charges.

33. **Question:** What term describes the ability of an organism to survive and reproduce in its environment?

- A) Adaptability
- B) Fitness
- C) Resilience
- D) Hardiness

    Answer: B) Fitness

Explanation: In evolutionary biology, fitness describes an organism's ability to survive and reproduce in its environment. Higher fitness organisms are more likely to pass on their genes to the next generation.

34. **Question:** What type of rock is formed by the cooling and solidifying of magma or lava?

- A) Metamorphic rock
- B) Sedimentary rock
- C) Igneous rock
- D) Fossil rock

Answer: C) Igneous rock

Explanation: Igneous rock is formed through the cooling and solidification of magma or lava. It can form beneath the Earth's surface, or on the surface when volcanoes erupt.

35. **Question:** What does the pH scale measure?

- A) The concentration of salt in a solution
- B) The concentration of hydrogen ions in a solution
- C) The temperature of a solution
- D) The amount of sugar in a solution

Answer: B) The concentration of hydrogen ions in a solution

Explanation: The pH scale measures the concentration of hydrogen ions (H+) in a solution. A lower pH indicates a higher concentration of H+ ions and a more acidic solution, while a higher pH indicates a lower concentration of H+ ions and a more basic or alkaline solution.

36. **Question:** What is the function of white blood cells in the human body?

- A) To carry oxygen to body tissues
- B) To clot blood
- C) To fight infections
- D) To produce hormones

Answer: C) To fight infections

Explanation: White blood cells, or leukocytes, play a crucial role in the immune system. They help the body fight off infections by attacking bacteria, viruses, and other pathogens.

37. **Question:** What is the name of our galaxy?

- A) Andromeda
- B) Milky Way
- C) Orion
- D) Alpha Centauri

Answer: B) Milky Way

Explanation: The galaxy that includes our solar system is called the Milky Way. It is a barred spiral galaxy, and it's one of billions of galaxies in the universe.

38. **Question:** What type of mirror causes parallel light rays to converge to a focus?

- A) Plane mirror
- B) Convex mirror
- C) Concave mirror
- D) Prism mirror

    Answer: C) Concave mirror

Explanation: Concave mirrors, or converging mirrors, reflect light inward to one focal point. They are used in various applications, including telescopes, headlights, and shaving mirrors.

39. **Question:** In what process do plants convert light energy from the sun into chemical energy?

- A) Respiration
- B) Transpiration
- C) Photosynthesis
- D) Fermentation

Answer: C) Photosynthesis

Explanation: In the process of photosynthesis, plants convert light energy from the sun into chemical energy in the form of glucose, which can be used by the plant for growth and reproduction.

40. **Question:** What is the smallest unit of life that can function independently?

- A) Molecule
- B) Organism
- C) Cell
- D) Tissue

Answer: C) Cell

Explanation: The cell is the smallest unit of life that can function independently. Cells can perform all the necessary functions of life, including taking in nutrients, converting nutrients into energy, carrying out specialized functions, and reproducing as necessary.

41. **Question:** What is the change in state from a gas directly to a solid called?

- A) Sublimation

- B) Deposition
- C) Condensation
- D) Evaporation

    Answer: B) Deposition

Explanation: Deposition, also known as desublimation, is the change of state from a gas directly to a solid, skipping the liquid state.

42. **Question:** What part of the atom carries a positive charge?
- A) Electron
- B) Neutron
- C) Proton
- D) Nucleus

    Answer: C) Proton

Explanation: Protons, which are located in the nucleus of an atom, carry a positive charge. The number of protons in an atom determines its atomic number and identifies the type of element it is.

43. **Question:** What is the principle by which birds and airplanes are able to achieve lift?
- A) Newton's First Law of Motion

- B) Bernoulli's Principle
- C) Pascal's Principle
- D) Archimedes' Principle

Answer: B) Bernoulli's Principle

Explanation: Bernoulli's Principle explains that as the speed of a moving fluid (such as air) increases, its pressure decreases. This principle is key in explaining how birds and airplanes achieve lift.

44. **Question:** What part of the plant is responsible for photosynthesis?

- A) Roots
- B) Stem
- C) Leaves
- D) Flowers

Answer: C) Leaves

Explanation: The leaves of a plant are primarily responsible for photosynthesis. They contain a pigment called chlorophyll, which captures light energy from the sun and begins the process of converting it into chemical energy.

45. **Question:** What causes the phases of the moon?

- A) The rotation of the Earth
- B) The reflection of sunlight off the moon's surface
- C) The shadow of the Earth falling on the moon
- D) The rotation of the moon

Answer: B) The reflection of sunlight off the moon's surface

Explanation: The phases of the moon are caused by the changing angles of the sun, moon, and Earth, and how much of the moon's surface reflects sunlight back to us. It's not caused by the Earth's shadow (that would be a lunar eclipse).

46. **Question:** What is the main gas found in the air we breathe?

- A) Oxygen
- B) Nitrogen
- C) Carbon dioxide
- D) Helium

Answer: B) Nitrogen

Explanation: While oxygen is vital for most forms of life, the majority of the air we breathe is actually nitrogen. Approximately 78% of Earth's atmosphere is nitrogen, while oxygen makes up around 21%.

47. **Question:** What is the basic structural and functional unit of the nervous system?

- A) Axon
- B) Neuron
- C) Synapse
- D) Dendrite

Answer: B) Neuron

Explanation: The neuron is the basic structural and functional unit of the nervous system. It's responsible for receiving sensory input from the external world, sending motor commands to our muscles, and transforming and relaying the electrical signals at every step in between.

48. **Question:** What term describes the measure of the amount of matter in an object?

- A) Weight
- B) Volume
- C) Density
- D) Mass

Answer: D) Mass

Explanation: Mass is a measure of the amount of matter in an object. It is usually measured in units like grams or kilograms. Unlike weight, mass does not change with location, even when the force of gravity changes.

49. **Question:** What type of chemical bond shares electron pairs between atoms?

- A) Ionic bond
- B) Covalent bond
- C) Metallic bond
- D) Hydrogen bond

    Answer: B) Covalent bond

Explanation: A covalent bond is a type of chemical bond that involves the sharing of electron pairs between atoms. These electron pairs are known as shared pairs or bonding pairs, and the stable balance of attractive and repulsive forces between atoms, when they share electrons, is known as covalent bonding.

50. **Question:** Which planet is known as the "Red Planet"?

- A) Venus
- B) Mars
- C) Jupiter
- D) Saturn

Answer: B) Mars

Explanation: Mars is often referred to as the "Red Planet" because its iron-rich dust gives the planet's surface a reddish appearance. This is particularly noticeable when Mars is viewed from space.

These questions are just a small sample of what you may encounter on the ASVAB General Science section. Keep practicing and reviewing relevant topics to get more comfortable with the kind of content you will see on the actual test. Remember, understanding the concepts is more important than memorizing facts, as it allows you to adapt your knowledge to any question you might face. Keep going, and you will be well-prepared for your ASVAB test!

General Science Test Strategies

Before you sit for the General Science subtest of the ASVAB, it's beneficial to have a test-taking strategy in place. By using smart strategies, you'll be better equipped to handle the wide range of topics the test covers, manage your time effectively, and approach difficult questions with confidence.

1. **Understand the test structure:** The General Science subtest contains 16 questions which must be answered in 8 minutes if you're taking the computer-delivered test, or 25 questions in 11 minutes if you're taking the pencil-and-paper test. The questions are all multiple choice and cover a wide range of general science topics. Understanding the structure of the test will help you manage your time effectively and know what to expect.

2. **Review major science topics:** The General Science subtest covers a wide range of topics, including biology, chemistry, physics, and earth and space science. Make sure you have a solid grasp of the basics in each of these areas. While you don't need to be an expert, understanding key concepts, principles, and vocabulary can make a significant difference.

3. **Time management is crucial:** With less than a minute per question, time management is vital. Avoid spending too long on any one question. If you encounter a question that seems particularly difficult, don't hesitate to skip it and return to it later if time allows.

4. **Use the process of elimination:** With four possible answers for each question, you can often eliminate one or two choices that are clearly incorrect. By doing so, you improve your odds of selecting the correct answer, even if you're not entirely sure.

5. **Read each question carefully:** This may seem obvious, but under the pressure of the test, it's easy to misread or misunderstand a question. Make sure to read each question and all the answer choices carefully. Look out for negative wording (such as "which of the following is NOT...") and make sure you're answering what the question is actually asking.

6. **Don't leave blanks:** There's no penalty for guessing on the ASVAB, so make sure to answer every question, even if you're unsure. If you're

stuck, use the process of elimination to improve your chances, and then make your best guess.

7. **Practice, practice, practice:** One of the best ways to prepare for the ASVAB General Science subtest is by taking practice tests. These can help you get a feel for the types of questions that will be asked, the pace you need to maintain, and the process of eliminating incorrect answer choices.

8. **Relax and maintain a positive mindset:** Test anxiety can negatively impact performance. Be sure to get a good night's sleep before the test, eat a healthy meal beforehand, and take deep breaths if you start to feel overwhelmed during the test. Remember, it's okay not to know every answer. Just do your best and keep a positive mindset.

By following these strategies, you'll be well on your way to tackling the General Science subtest of the ASVAB with confidence. Best of luck with your preparations!

Chapter 3
Arithmetic Reasoning

Overview and Study Guide

The Arithmetic Reasoning subtest is one of the ten subtests of the Armed Services Vocational Aptitude Battery (ASVAB). It is one of the four subtests used to compute the Armed Forces Qualification Test (AFQT) score, which determines eligibility for enlistment in the U.S. military. This chapter provides an overview of the Arithmetic Reasoning subtest and offers a study guide to help you prepare for this important exam.

Overview

The Arithmetic Reasoning subtest measures your ability to solve arithmetic word problems, which you would encounter on a regular basis in a high school math class. The questions are multiple-choice and cover a variety of math topics including fractions, percentages, ratios, interest rates, linear equations, and number sequences.

On the computer-delivered test, you will have 39 minutes to answer 16 questions, whereas on the paper-and-pencil test, you will have 36 minutes to answer 30 questions. All the questions are word problems and require the application of reasoning skills to solve.

Study Guide

1. Review Basic Arithmetic Skills: The Arithmetic Reasoning subtest requires a solid understanding of basic arithmetic. Brush up on addition, subtraction, multiplication, and division of both whole numbers and fractions. Remember to also review concepts like percentages, ratios, and averages.

2. Practice Word Problems: This subtest primarily consists of word problems. Practice problems that require multiple steps to solve, and pay attention to key words and phrases that indicate what kind of mathematical operation you need to use.

3. Understand Ratios and Proportions: Ratios and proportions are a common part of the Arithmetic Reasoning subtest. Practice setting up and solving proportions, and make sure you understand how to interpret ratios in various forms (3:1, 3 to 1, 3/1).

4. Work on Algebraic Problems: Some questions may require basic algebra skills, like solving equations for an unknown variable. Make sure you're comfortable with concepts like isolating variables, dealing with negative numbers, and solving linear equations.

5. Brush Up on Geometry: While not as common, some questions might involve basic geometric concepts, such as understanding the properties of different shapes and how to calculate area and volume.

6. Learn to Work Efficiently: Because time can be an issue, it's important to practice working efficiently. This means learning to quickly identify what a question is asking and what steps are necessary to arrive at the answer.

7. Take Practice Tests: Practice tests are one of the most effective ways to prepare for the ASVAB. Not only will they help you become familiar with the format and time constraints of the test, but they'll also let you see what areas you need to focus on in your studies.

To excel in the Arithmetic Reasoning subtest, it's important to not only have the necessary mathematical skills, but also to employ effective test-taking strategies. Here are some key strategies to use when you take the test:

1. Break down complex problems: Some word problems may initially seem complex, but can become manageable if broken down into smaller parts. Identify what the question is asking and then determine the steps you need to take to find the answer.

2. Identify the operation: Each word problem requires a mathematical operation - addition, subtraction, multiplication, or division. Words like 'total', 'combined', or 'in all' suggest addition, while words like 'difference', 'fewer', or 'remain' imply subtraction. 'Times', 'product', 'every', or 'at this rate' indicate multiplication, while 'per', 'out of', 'ratio of', or 'quotient' suggest division. Recognizing these key words can help you understand which operation to use.

3. Use the process of elimination: Just like in other subtests, the process of elimination is a useful strategy in the Arithmetic Reasoning section. If you're unsure about an answer, try to eliminate the choices that seem incorrect. This narrows down your options and increases your chances of guessing the correct answer.

4. Draw diagrams for geometry problems: If you encounter a geometry problem, drawing a simple diagram can help visualize the problem and make it easier to solve.

5. Watch the clock: Keep an eye on the time. It's crucial to maintain a steady pace throughout the test - not rushing, but not lagging either. If a question is taking too long to solve, it may be best to make an educated guess and move on.

6. Double-check your work: If time permits, it's always a good idea to double-check your answers. Even simple arithmetic can sometimes trip you up, especially when you're under time pressure.

7. Practice mental math: While you should use scratch paper when necessary, honing your mental math skills can save you time and help you work more efficiently.

Remember that while studying and understanding concepts is crucial, incorporating these strategies into your test-taking approach can make a significant difference in your ASVAB score.

By following this study guide and practicing regularly, you can improve your skills and confidence in preparation for the Arithmetic Reasoning subtest of the ASVAB. Remember, consistent practice and thorough preparation are the keys to success. Good luck with your studies!

Practice Test with Answers

1. Question: John has 3 times as many apples as Tom. If Tom has 15 apples, how many apples does John have?

- A) 30
- B) 45
- C) 60
- D) 75

Answer: B) 45

Explanation: John has 3 times as many apples as Tom, so he has 3 * 15 = 45 apples.

2. Question: A train travels at a speed of 60 miles per hour. How far does the train travel in 2.5 hours?

- A) 120 miles
- B) 150 miles

- C) 180 miles
- D) 210 miles

Answer: B) 150 miles

Explanation: Distance = speed * time, so the train travels 60 * 2.5 = 150 miles.

3. Question: If 5 shirts cost $125, how much does each shirt cost?

- A) $20
- B) $25
- C) $30
- D) $35

Answer: B) $25

Explanation: Each shirt costs $125 / 5 = $25.

4. Question: What is 25% of 200?

- A) 25
- B) 50
- C) 75
- D) 100

Answer: B) 50

Explanation: 25% of 200 is 0.25 * 200 = 50.

5. Question: A group of people collected 120 cans for recycling. If they collected the same amount each day for 4 days, how many cans did they collect each day?

- A) 20 cans
- B) 30 cans
- C) 40 cans
- D) 50 cans

Answer: B) 30 cans

Explanation: Each day they collected 120 / 4 = 30 cans.

6. Question: If a car gets 30 miles per gallon, how many miles can it travel on 10 gallons of gas?

- A) 100 miles
- B) 200 miles
- C) 300 miles
- D) 400 miles

Answer: C) 300 miles

Explanation: The car can travel 30 * 10 = 300 miles on 10 gallons of gas.

7. Question: A rectangular garden is 12 feet long and 10 feet wide. What is the area of the garden?

- A) 100 square feet
- B) 110 square feet
- C) 120 square feet
- D) 130 square feet

Answer: C) 120 square feet

Explanation: The area of a rectangle is length * width, so the area of the garden is 12 * 10 = 120 square feet.

8. Question: A store sells 24 packs of soda for $12. How much does each pack cost?

- A) $0.25
- B) $0.50
- C) $0.75
- D) $1.00

Answer: B) $0.50

Explanation: Each pack of soda costs $12 / 24 = $0.50.

9. Question: A car travels 420 miles on 14 gallons of gas. What is the car's miles-per-gallon?

- A) 20 mpg
- B) 30 mpg
- C) 40 mpg
- D) 50 mpg

Answer: B) 30 mpg

Explanation: The car's miles-per-gallon is 420 / 14 = 30 mpg.

10. Question: A bag contains 4 red balls, 3 green balls, and 2 blue balls. What fraction of the balls are blue?

- A) 1/4
- B) 1/3
- C) 2/9
- D) 1/2

Answer: C) 2/9

Explanation: There are a total of 4 + 3 + 2 = 9 balls, and 2 of them are blue, so the fraction that are blue is 2 / 9.

11. Question: If a box contains 12 candies and Sally eats 3, how many candies are left in the box?

- A) 9
- B) 10
- C) 11
- D) 12

Answer: A) 9

Explanation: After Sally eats 3 candies, there are 12 - 3 = 9 candies left.

12. Question: Tom earns $15 per hour. How much does he earn for 8 hours of work?

- A) $90
- B) $120
- C) $150
- D) $180

Answer: C) $150

Explanation: Tom earns $15 * 8 = $120 for 8 hours of work.

13. Question: A store offers a 20% discount on a coat that originally costs $120. What is the sale price of the coat?

- A) $96
- B) $100
- C) $104
- D) $108

Answer: A) $96

Explanation: The amount of the discount is 20% * $120 = $24. So, the sale price of the coat is $120 - $24 = $96.

14. Question: What is the average of the numbers 10, 15, and 20?

- A) 13
- B) 15
- C) 17
- D) 18

Answer: B) 15

Explanation: The average of the numbers is (10 + 15 + 20) / 3 = 15.

15. Question: If a bicycle travels at a speed of 10 miles per hour, how far does it travel in 30 minutes?

- A) 3 miles
- B) 5 miles
- C) 7 miles
- D) 10 miles

Answer: B) 5 miles

Explanation: The bicycle travels at 10 miles per hour, so in half an hour (30 minutes), it travels 10 / 2 = 5 miles.

16. Question: If 6 workers can build 6 cars in 6 days, how long would it take 3 workers to build 3 cars?

- A) 3 days
- B) 6 days
- C) 9 days
- D) 12 days

Answer: B) 6 days

Explanation: According to the problem, 1 worker can build 1 car in 6 days. Therefore, 3 workers can build 3 cars in the same amount of time, 6 days.

17. Question: A recipe calls for 2 cups of flour to make 16 cookies. How much flour is needed to make 48 cookies?

- A) 4 cups
- B) 6 cups
- C) 8 cups
- D) 10 cups

Answer: C) 6 cups

Explanation: The amount of flour needed is proportional to the number of cookies. If 2 cups of flour make 16 cookies, then to make 48 cookies (which is 3 times more), you need 2 * 3 = 6 cups of flour.

18. Question: A car travels 200 miles in 4 hours. What is the average speed of the car in miles per hour?

- A) 40 mph
- B) 50 mph
- C) 60 mph
- D) 70 mph

Answer: A) 50 mph

Explanation: The average speed of the car is 200 miles / 4 hours = 50 mph.

19. Question: John has $150 and wants to buy video games that cost $25 each. How many video games can John buy?

- A) 5
- B) 6
- C) 7
- D) 8

Answer: B) 6

Explanation: John can buy $150 / $25 = 6 video games.

20. Question: If a water tank holds 500 liters of water and is already 3/5 full, how much more water is needed to fill the tank?

- A) 100 liters
- B) 200 liters
- C) 300 liters
- D) 400 liters

Answer: B) 200 liters

Explanation: The tank already contains 3/5 * 500 = 300 liters of water. So, 500 - 300 = 200 liters of water are needed to fill the tank.

21. Question: A library has 300 books. If 1/5 of the books are fiction, how many fiction books are there in the library?

- A) 50
- B) 60
- C) 70
- D) 80

Answer: B) 60

Explanation: The number of fiction books in the library is 1/5 * 300 = 60.

22. Question: Tom wants to save $150 for a new gadget. If he saves $15 each week, how many weeks will it take for him to save enough money?

- A) 8 weeks
- B) 10 weeks
- C) 12 weeks
- D) 15 weeks

Answer: B) 10 weeks

Explanation: It will take Tom $150 / $15 = 10 weeks to save enough money.

23. Question: If a triangle has a base of 10 cm and a height of 15 cm, what is its area?

- A) 50 sq cm
- B) 75 sq cm
- C) 100 sq cm
- D) 125 sq cm

Answer: B) 75 sq cm

Explanation: The area of a triangle is 1/2 * base * height. So, the area is 1/2 * 10 * 15 = 75 square cm.

24. Question: A car uses 4 gallons of gas to travel 120 miles. How many gallons of gas would the car use to travel 300 miles?

- A) 7 gallons
- B) 10 gallons
- C) 12 gallons
- D) 15 gallons

Answer: B) 10 gallons

Explanation: The car travels 120 miles / 4 gallons = 30 miles per gallon. Therefore, it would use 300 miles / 30 mpg = 10 gallons to travel 300 miles.

25. Question: If a shirt is on sale for 25% off and the original price was $40, what is the sale price?

- A) $20
- B) $25
- C) $30
- D) $35

Answer: C) $30

Explanation: The discount is 25% * $40 = $10. So, the sale price is $40 - $10 = $30.

26. Question: If a box of cereal serves 12 and there are 6 people in a family, how many servings are left after the family has breakfast?

- A) 2
- B) 4
- C) 6
- D) 8

Answer: C) 6

Explanation: After the family has breakfast, there are 12 - 6 = 6 servings left.

27. Question: A painter can paint a room in 4 hours. How long will it take for two painters to paint the same room working together?

- A) 1 hour
- B) 2 hours
- C) 3 hours
- D) 4 hours

Answer: B) 2 hours

Explanation: If two painters work together, they can paint the room in 4 hours / 2 = 2 hours.

28. Question: If a rectangle has a length of 8 cm and a width of 3 cm, what is its perimeter?

- A) 14 cm
- B) 22 cm
- C) 24 cm
- D) 30 cm

Answer: B) 22 cm

Explanation: The perimeter of a rectangle is 2 * (length + width). So, the perimeter is 2 * (8 + 3) = 22 cm.

29. Question: A factory produces 500 widgets in 10 hours. How many widgets does the factory produce per hour?

- A) 25
- B) 50
- C) 75
- D) 100

Answer: B) 50

Explanation: The factory produces 500 widgets / 10 hours = 50 widgets per hour.

30. Question: A bike costs $200 and is on sale for 15% off. What is the sale price of the bike?

- A) $170
- B) $180
- C) $185
- D) $190

Answer: A) $170

Explanation: The discount is 15% * $200 = $30. So, the sale price is $200 - $30 = $170.

31. Question: A store has 80 apples. If it sells 3/4 of them, how many apples are left?

- A) 10
- B) 20
- C) 30
- D) 40

Answer: B) 20

Explanation: The store sells 3/4 * 80 = 60 apples, so there are 80 - 60 = 20 apples left.

32. Question: A car travels 360 miles on a tank of gas that holds 12 gallons. How many miles does the car get per gallon?

- A) 25 mpg
- B) 30 mpg
- C) 35 mpg
- D) 40 mpg

Answer: C) 30 mpg

Explanation: The car gets 360 miles / 12 gallons = 30 miles per gallon.

33. Question: A loaf of bread is sliced into 20 pieces. If a family eats 1/4 of the loaf for breakfast, how many slices are left?

- A) 10
- B) 12
- C) 15
- D) 18

Answer: C) 15

Explanation: The family eats 1/4 * 20 = 5 slices, so there are 20 - 5 = 15 slices left.

34. Question: If you buy 3 books at $12 each, what will be the total cost?

- A) $24
- B) $36
- C) $48
- D) $60

Answer: B) $36

Explanation: The total cost would be 3 * $12 = $36.

35. Question: If a rectangle has a length of 5 meters and a width of 3 meters, what is its area?

- A) 8 sq m
- B) 12 sq m
- C) 15 sq m
- D) 18 sq m

Answer: C) 15 sq m

Explanation: The area of a rectangle is length * width. So, the area is 5 * 3 = 15 square meters.

36. Question: A printer can print 15 pages in 3 minutes. How many pages can it print in one hour?

- A) 100
- B) 200
- C) 300
- D) 400

Answer: B) 300

Explanation: The printer can print 15 pages / 3 minutes = 5 pages per minute. So, in one hour (which is 60 minutes), it can print 5 * 60 = 300 pages.

37. Question: If a jacket costs $60 and is on sale for 20% off, what is the sale price?

- A) $36

- B) $48
- C) $50
- D) $52

Answer: B) $48

Explanation: The discount is 20% * $60 = $12. So, the sale price is $60 - $12 = $48.

38. Question: A car can travel 480 miles on a 16-gallon tank of gas. What is its fuel efficiency in miles per gallon?

- A) 20 mpg
- B) 25 mpg
- C) 30 mpg
- D) 40 mpg

Answer: C) 30 mpg

Explanation: The car's fuel efficiency is 480 miles / 16 gallons = 30 miles per gallon.

39. Question: A soccer team won 18 games out of a 24-game season. What percentage of games did they win?

- A) 65%

- B) 70%
- C) 75%
- D) 80%

Answer: C) 75%

Explanation: The team won 18 / 24 = 0.75 of its games, which is 75%.

40. Question: A store sells shirts for $20 each. If a customer buys 3 shirts, what will be the total cost?

- A) $40
- B) $60
- C) $80
- D) $100

Answer: B) $60

Explanation: The total cost would be 3 * $20 = $60.

41. Question: A recipe calls for 2 cups of sugar to make a cake. If you want to make 1/2 of the cake, how much sugar do you need?

- A) 0.5 cup
- B) 1 cup
- C) 1.5 cups

- D) 2 cups

Answer: B) 1 cup

Explanation: If you are making 1/2 of the cake, you need 1/2 of the sugar, which is 1/2 * 2 = 1 cup of sugar.

42. Question: A school bus can carry 50 students. If 3/5 of the seats are occupied, how many students are on the bus?

- A) 20
- B) 30
- C) 40
- D) 50

Answer: B) 30

Explanation: If 3/5 of the seats are occupied, then there are 3/5 * 50 = 30 students on the bus.

43. Question: If you read 4 chapters of a book in 2 hours, how many chapters can you read in 5 hours?

- A) 6 chapters
- B) 8 chapters
- C) 10 chapters

- D) 12 chapters

Answer: C) 10 chapters

Explanation: You read at a rate of 4 chapters / 2 hours = 2 chapters per hour. Therefore, in 5 hours, you can read 2 * 5 = 10 chapters.

44. Question: A train travels 600 miles in 8 hours. What is the train's average speed?

- A) 60 mph
- B) 70 mph
- C) 75 mph
- D) 80 mph

Answer: D) 75 mph

Explanation: The train's average speed is 600 miles / 8 hours = 75 miles per hour.

45. Question: If a sweater costs $50 and is on sale for 20% off, what is the sale price?

- A) $30
- B) $35
- C) $40
- D) $45

Answer: C) $40

Explanation: The discount is 20% * $50 = $10. So, the sale price is $50 - $10 = $40.

46. Question: A pizza is sliced into 8 pieces. If a family eats 3/4 of the pizza, how many slices are left?

- A) 1
- B) 2
- C) 3
- D) 4

Answer: B) 2

Explanation: The family eats 3/4 * 8 = 6 slices, so there are 8 - 6 = 2 slices left.

47. Question: If a rectangle has a length of 6 meters and a width of 4 meters, what is its perimeter?

- A) 16 meters
- B) 20 meters
- C) 24 meters
- D) 28 meters

Answer: B) 20 meters

Explanation: The perimeter of a rectangle is 2 * (length + width). So, the perimeter is 2 * (6 + 4) = 20 meters.

48. Question: A cyclist can travel 25 kilometers in an hour. How far can they travel in 3.5 hours?

- A) 75 kilometers
- B) 87.5 kilometers
- C) 100 kilometers
- D) 112.5 kilometers

Answer: B) 87.5 kilometers

Explanation: The cyclist can travel 25 kilometers per hour * 3.5 hours = 87.5 kilometers.

49. Question: A shirt costs $30 and is on sale for 15% off. What is the sale price of the shirt?

- A) $20
- B) $25
- C) $25.5
- D) $26

Answer: C) $25.5

Explanation: The discount is 15% * $30 = $4.5. So, the sale price is $30 - $4.5 = $25.5.

50. Question: A car travels 350 miles on a tank of gas that holds 10 gallons. How many miles does the car get per gallon?

- A) 30 mpg
- B) 35 mpg
- C) 40 mpg
- D) 45 mpg

Answer: B) 35 mpg

Explanation: The car gets 350 miles / 10 gallons = 35 miles per gallon.

Arithmetic Reasoning Test Strategies

Arithmetic Reasoning is a critical section of the ASVAB as it assesses your ability to solve mathematical problems using reasoning. These problems are not straightforward and require some logical deduction to find the solution. Hence, it's essential to strategize your approach for this section.

Understanding the Question Format

The Arithmetic Reasoning section is presented in the form of word problems. These problems typically provide a scenario, ask a question about the scenario, and offer multiple-choice answers. Understanding the format of the questions will enable you to break down each problem and help identify the relevant information.

Time Management

The Arithmetic Reasoning section consists of 30 questions which need to be answered within 36 minutes. This means, on average, you have just over a minute to answer each question. It's important to pace yourself to avoid rushing through the last few questions. Remember, unanswered questions are counted as incorrect on the ASVAB.

Break Down the Problem

A practical approach is to break down the problem into smaller, manageable parts. Identify the knowns and unknowns in the problem and what operation (addition, subtraction, multiplication, division) you need to use to find the answer.

Estimate

Use estimation when it can help you eliminate one or more answer choices. This can often speed up your problem-solving process. Remember, your goal is to answer correctly, but also to do it efficiently.

Check Your Work

If you find yourself with extra time, it's always a good idea to go back and check your work. Even the simplest of arithmetic problems can involve steps where errors can occur, and rechecking your work can often help you catch these mistakes before they cost you valuable points.

Skip Difficult Questions

If a question seems too difficult or time-consuming, it might be a good idea to skip it and move on to the next one. You can always come back to it later if you have time. Remember, all questions are weighted equally, so it's better to answer more straightforward questions correctly than to get stuck on a challenging one and run out of time.

Practice Regularly

The more you practice, the better your mathematical reasoning will get, and the quicker you'll become at recognizing what type of problem you're dealing with and how to solve it. Regular practice can also help reduce anxiety and improve your confidence on the day of the test.

Keep in mind that the Arithmetic Reasoning section of the ASVAB is not just about your ability to do math—it's about your ability to solve problems. With good strategies and plenty of practice, you'll be well-prepared to tackle this section of the test.

Chapter 4
Word Knowledge

Overview and Study Guide

The Word Knowledge section of the ASVAB is designed to examine your vocabulary, verbal expression, and ability to understand and interpret written content. In other words, it's a measure of your language skills and understanding of English. This portion of the test consists of 35 questions that must be answered within 11 minutes, making time a crucial factor.

In this section, you will encounter multiple-choice questions that present a word in capital letters, followed by four answer options. Your task is to identify the option that most closely matches the meaning of the given word. In some cases, you may also be asked to find the word that has the opposite meaning.

Study Guide

Studying for the Word Knowledge section of the ASVAB involves building a strong vocabulary and understanding of English language conventions. Here are some strategies to guide your preparation:

1. Expand Your Vocabulary:

To do well in this section, you'll need a broad vocabulary. Regular reading is one of the most effective ways to learn new words. Reading a variety of material, from novels to newspapers, can expose you to different words used in various contexts.

2. Use a Dictionary:

Whenever you come across a word you don't understand, look it up in a dictionary. Try to understand its meaning, usage, and synonyms. It can also be helpful to write down the word and its definition to reinforce your memory.

3. Learn Root Words, Prefixes, and Suffixes:

Understanding the common root words, prefixes, and suffixes in English can help you make educated guesses about unfamiliar words. For example, if you know 'bio-' means life and '-logy' means study of, you can infer that 'biology' is the study of life.

4. Practice Synonyms and Antonyms:

Many questions in this section ask you to identify synonyms (words with similar meanings) and antonyms (words with opposite meanings). Practice identifying these in your reading, or use flashcards to test your knowledge.

5. Use the Word in a Sentence:

When you learn a new word, try to use it in a sentence. This helps you understand the word's context and reinforces its meaning in your mind.

6. Take Practice Tests:

Practice tests can help familiarize you with the format of the Word Knowledge section and the type of questions you'll encounter. They can also help you gauge your progress and identify areas for improvement.

Remember, improving your vocabulary is a gradual process. Consistent practice, reading, and testing of your knowledge will yield improvements over time. With a solid preparation strategy and plenty of practice, you'll be well-equipped to tackle the Word Knowledge section of the ASVAB.

Word Knowledge Practice Test with Answers

1. Question: COMPETENT

- A) unskilled
- B) unfit
- C) capable
- D) lazy

Answer: C) capable

Explanation: 'Competent' means having the necessary ability, knowledge, or skill to do something successfully, which aligns closely with 'capable'.

2. Question: BENEVOLENT

- A) kind
- B) cruel
- C) selfish
- D) poor

Answer: A) kind

Explanation: 'Benevolent' means well-meaning and kindly, which makes 'kind' the most suitable synonym.

3. Question: JOVIAL

- A) sad
- B) gloomy
- C) cheerful

- D) angry

Answer: C) cheerful

Explanation: 'Jovial' means cheerful and friendly, so the closest synonym is 'cheerful'.

4. Question: RANCOR

- A) peace
- B) bitterness
- C) harmony
- D) happiness

Answer: B) bitterness

Explanation: 'Rancor' refers to long-standing bitterness or resentfulness, making 'bitterness' the closest match.

5. Question: DEPLETE

- A) fill
- B) enrich
- C) drain
- D) improve

Answer: C) drain

Explanation: 'Deplete' means to use up the supply or resources of something, aligning closely with 'drain'.

6. Question: IMPERATIVE

- A) optional
- B) necessary
- C) unimportant
- D) unnecessary

Answer: B) necessary

7. Question: OBSOLETE

- A) current
- B) outdated
- C) modern
- D) new

Answer: B) outdated

8. Question: DILIGENT

- A) lazy
- B) hardworking
- C) carefree
- D) reckless

Answer: B) hardworking

9. Question: FICTITIOUS

- A) real
- B) imaginary
- C) historical
- D) factual

Answer: B) imaginary

10. Question: ENIGMA

- A) solution
- B) mystery
- C) clarity
- D) openness

Answer: B) mystery

11. Question: SPORADIC

- A) regular
- B) occasional
- C) constant
- D) perpetual

Answer: B) occasional

Explanation: 'Sporadic' means occurring at irregular intervals or only in a few places; scattered or isolated, which is similar in meaning to 'occasional'.

12. Question: NOVEL

- A) common
- B) usual
- C) new
- D) ordinary

Answer: C) new

Explanation: 'Novel' in this context means new or unusual in an interesting way.

13. Question: SUPERFICIAL

- A) deep
- B) profound
- C) shallow
- D) serious

Answer: C) shallow

Explanation: 'Superficial' means existing or occurring at or on the surface, hence 'shallow' is the most suitable synonym.

14. Question: HOSTILITY

- A) peace
- B) friendship
- C) anger
- D) joy

Answer: C) anger

Explanation: 'Hostility' refers to unfriendly or aggressive behavior or attitudes, which aligns closely with 'anger'.

15. Question: AMBIGUOUS

- A) clear
- B) vague
- C) certain
- D) obvious

Answer: B) vague

Explanation: 'Ambiguous' means open to more than one interpretation; having a double meaning, making 'vague' the closest match.

16. Question: VERACITY

- A) dishonesty

- B) truthfulness
- C) deceit
- D) fallacy

Answer: B) truthfulness

Explanation: 'Veracity' means conformity to facts; accuracy, and also habitual truthfulness, hence 'truthfulness' is the best match.

17. Question: ABUNDANT

- A) scarce
- B) rare
- C) plentiful
- D) lacking

Answer: C) plentiful

Explanation: 'Abundant' means existing or available in large quantities; plentiful.

18. Question: PERSISTENT

- A) fleeting
- B) temporary
- C) enduring
- D) short-lived

Answer: C) enduring

Explanation: 'Persistent' means continuing firmly or obstinately in an opinion or course of action in spite of difficulty or opposition. 'Enduring' is the closest synonym.

19. Question: BREVITY

- A) length
- B) verbosity
- C) conciseness
- D) expansion

Answer: C) conciseness

Explanation: 'Brevity' refers to concise and exact use of words in writing or speech, hence 'conciseness' is the best match.

20. Question: MALEVOLENT

- A) kind
- B) benevolent
- C) malicious
- D) gentle

Answer: C) malicious

Explanation: 'Malevolent' means having or showing a wish to do evil to others, so 'malicious' is the closest synonym.

21. Question: ABSTAIN

- A) indulge
- B) partake
- C) refrain
- D) engage

Answer: C) refrain

Explanation: 'Abstain' means to restrain oneself from doing or enjoying something, hence 'refrain' is the closest synonym.

22. Question: EXUBERANT

- A) subdued
- B) depressed
- C) energetic
- D) despondent

Answer: C) energetic

Explanation: 'Exuberant' means filled with or characterized by a lively energy and excitement, aligning closely with 'energetic'.

23. Question: MEAGER

- A) abundant
- B) bountiful
- C) scant
- D) copious

Answer: C) scant

Explanation: 'Meager' means lacking in quantity or quality, which makes 'scant' the most suitable synonym.

24. Question: DIVERSE

- A) similar
- B) identical
- C) varied
- D) uniform

Answer: C) varied

Explanation: 'Diverse' means showing a great deal of variety, so the closest synonym is 'varied'.

25. Question: INEPT

- A) skilled
- B) competent
- C) clumsy
- D) proficient

Answer: C) clumsy

Explanation: 'Inept' means having or showing no skill; clumsy.

26. Question: VIVID

- A) dull
- B) drab
- C) vibrant
- D) lifeless

Answer: C) vibrant

Explanation: 'Vivid' means producing powerful feelings or strong, clear images in the mind, or (of a color) intensely deep or bright, making 'vibrant' the closest match.

27. Question: PLAUSIBLE

- A) unbelievable

- B) credible
- C) improbable
- D) unlikely

Answer: B) credible

Explanation: 'Plausible' means seeming reasonable or probable, hence 'credible' is the most suitable synonym.

28. Question: CAUTIOUS

- A) reckless
- B) careful
- C) rash
- D) imprudent

Answer: B) careful

Explanation: 'Cautious' means careful to avoid potential problems or dangers, so 'careful' is the closest synonym.

29. Question: INSIPID

- A) tasty
- B) flavorless
- C) delicious

- D) savory

Answer: B) flavorless

Explanation: 'Insipid' means lacking flavor or zest; not tasty, making 'flavorless' the closest match.

30. Question: VIGILANT

- A) careless
- B) negligent
- C) watchful
- D) distracted

Answer: C) watchful

Explanation: 'Vigilant' means keeping careful watch for possible danger or difficulties, so 'watchful' is the closest synonym.

31. Question: GRANDIOSE

- A) simple
- B) modest
- C) extravagant
- D) humble

Answer: C) extravagant

Explanation: 'Grandiose' refers to something that is impressive or magnificent in appearance or style, especially pretentiously so, making 'extravagant' the closest match.

32. Question: DISPARAGE

- A) praise
- B) commend
- C) belittle
- D) glorify

Answer: C) belittle

Explanation: 'Disparage' means to regard or represent as being of little worth, hence 'belittle' is the closest synonym.

33. Question: VEX

- A) please
- B) soothe
- C) annoy
- D) comfort

Answer: C) annoy

Explanation: 'Vex' means to make someone feel annoyed, frustrated, or worried, aligning closely with 'annoy'.

34. Question: VOLATILE

- A) stable
- B) constant
- C) unpredictable
- D) unchanging

Answer: C) unpredictable

Explanation: 'Volatile' means liable to change rapidly and unpredictably, especially for the worse, which makes 'unpredictable' the most suitable synonym.

35. Question: ARTICULATE

- A) unclear
- B) vague
- C) expressive
- D) ambiguous

Answer: C) expressive

Explanation: 'Articulate' means having or showing the ability to speak fluently and coherently, so the closest synonym is 'expressive'.

36. Question: ERRATIC

- A) consistent
- B) regular
- C) unpredictable
- D) steady

Answer: C) unpredictable

Explanation: 'Erratic' means not even or regular in pattern or movement; unpredictable.

37. Question: LUCID

- A) unclear
- B) cloudy
- C) clear
- D) confusing

Answer: C) clear

Explanation: 'Lucid' means expressed clearly; easy to understand, making 'clear' the closest match.

38. Question: TACITURN

- A) talkative
- B) chatty
- C) quiet
- D) verbose

Answer: C) quiet

Explanation: 'Taciturn' means (of a person) reserved or uncommunicative in speech; saying little, hence 'quiet' is the most suitable synonym.

39. Question: FRUGAL

- A) wasteful
- B) spendthrift
- C) thrifty
- D) prodigal

Answer: C) thrifty

Explanation: 'Frugal' means sparing or economical with regard to money or food, so 'thrifty' is the closest synonym.

40. Question: REVERE

- A) disrespect
- B) scorn

- C) honor
- D) despise

Answer: C) honor

Explanation: 'Revere' means to feel deep respect or admiration for (something), making 'honor' the closest match.

41. Question: INDOLENT

- A) active
- B) energetic
- C) lazy
- D) industrious

Answer: C) lazy

Explanation: 'Indolent' means wanting to avoid activity or exertion; lazy.

42. Question: RECTIFY

- A) worsen
- B) exacerbate
- C) correct
- D) intensify

Answer: C) correct

Explanation: 'Rectify' means to make right; correct.

43. Question: JUBILANT

- A) unhappy
- B) sad
- C) ecstatic
- D) miserable

Answer: C) ecstatic

Explanation: 'Jubilant' means feeling or expressing great happiness and triumph. 'Ecstatic' is the closest synonym.

44. Question: TRANSGRESS

- A) obey
- B) follow
- C) violate
- D) comply

Answer: C) violate

Explanation: 'Transgress' means to go beyond the limits of what is morally, socially, or legally acceptable. 'Violate' is the closest synonym.

45. Question: DEPLETE

- A) replenish
- B) refill
- C) exhaust
- D) renew

Answer: C) exhaust

Explanation: 'Deplete' means to use up the supply or resources of something. 'Exhaust' is the closest synonym.

46. Question: TENACIOUS

- A) weak
- B) yielding
- C) persistent
- D) submissive

Answer: C) persistent

Explanation: 'Tenacious' means tending to keep a firm hold of something; clinging or adhering closely, which is close to the meaning of 'persistent'.

47. Question: EFFICACY

- A) ineffectiveness
- B) uselessness

- C) effectiveness
- D) impotence

Answer: C) effectiveness

Explanation: 'Efficacy' means the ability to produce a desired or intended result. 'Effectiveness' is the closest synonym.

48. Question: BENIGN

- A) harmful
- B) malignant
- C) kind
- D) malevolent

Answer: C) kind

Explanation: 'Benign' means gentle and kind, which is similar to 'kind'.

49. Question: VORACIOUS

- A) satiated
- B) full
- C) insatiable
- D) satisfied

Answer: C) insatiable

Explanation: 'Voracious' means wanting or devouring great quantities of food, or having a very eager approach to an activity. 'Insatiable' is the closest synonym.

50. Question: EPHEMERAL

- A) enduring
- B) lasting
- C) transient
- D) perpetual

Answer: C) transient

Explanation: 'Ephemeral' means lasting for a very short time, making 'transient' the closest match.

Word Knowledge Test Strategies

Word Knowledge is one of the most critical subtests of the ASVAB, as it tests your ability to understand, remember, and apply vocabulary. Here are some key strategies to keep in mind:

1. Understand the Structure of the Test:

In the Word Knowledge section, you are tested primarily on your understanding of synonyms. A word is provided in capital letters, and you must choose the answer that most closely matches the meaning of the given word. There are typically four options, and your task is to pick the one that you think is the closest in meaning to the word in question.

2. Develop a Strong Vocabulary:

The best way to prepare for this section is to develop a strong vocabulary. This can be achieved through regular reading, using vocabulary flashcards, and utilizing vocabulary-building applications and websites.

3. Utilize Context Clues:

If you come across a word you don't know, try to infer its meaning from context clues. Examine the structure of the word, including prefixes, root words, and suffixes. These can often give you a hint as to what the word means.

4. Practice Active Reading:

Active reading involves engaging with the text, questioning, predicting, and clarifying as you read. This can help improve your understanding and retention of vocabulary.

5. Take Regular Practice Tests:

Practice tests are a great way to familiarize yourself with the test format and question types. They can also help you identify areas where you might need to focus your studying. Remember to review not only the questions you got wrong but also the ones you got right. This will help reinforce the correct answers in your memory.

6. Develop a Strategy for Guessing:

In the Word Knowledge section, if you have no idea what the word means and can't infer it from context clues, your best bet is to make an educated guess. Eliminate any answer choices that you know are incorrect and choose from the remaining ones. Remember, there's no penalty for guessing on the ASVAB.

7. Stay Calm and Focused:

During the test, it's crucial to remain calm and not get stuck on a single question. If you're unsure, make your best guess, mark the question if that option is available, and move on. You can always come back to it later if time allows.

Remember, the key to acing the Word Knowledge subtest, as with any other section of the ASVAB, lies in thorough preparation and regular practice. By incorporating these strategies into your study plan, you'll be well on your way to achieving a high score.

Chapter 5
Paragraph Comprehension

Overview and Study Guide

The Paragraph Comprehension section of the ASVAB tests your ability to interpret and comprehend written information. This section, often considered part of the Verbal Expression score along with Word Knowledge, requires you to read passages and answer questions about the content accurately.

Understanding the Test Format:

The Paragraph Comprehension test includes 15 questions, and you have 13 minutes to complete it. The questions are multiple-choice, and each question is based on a brief passage. You'll need to use your comprehension skills to answer questions related to the main idea, supporting details, inferences, and the overall meaning of the passage.

Study Strategies and Tips:

1. **Active Reading:** Enhance your understanding by practicing active reading. This involves making notes, underlining or highlighting key points,

summarizing what you read, and asking questions about the text.

2. **Identify the Main Idea:** Every paragraph has a main idea or primary point. Often, the main idea is present in the first sentence (the topic sentence) of the paragraph. Other times, it's implied and must be inferred from the details given.

3. **Understand Supporting Details:** Supporting details provide more information about the main idea. They can include examples, descriptions, or explanations. Understanding these details can help you answer questions accurately.

4. **Make Inferences:** Sometimes, the answer isn't stated explicitly in the passage, and you'll have to make an inference. This involves using the information provided and your logic to deduce an unstated fact or conclusion.

5. **Summarize the Text:** After reading a passage, try summarizing it in your own words. This can help ensure you've understood the main points.

6. **Practice, Practice, Practice:** The best way to get good at paragraph comprehension is to practice.

Read a variety of texts, from news articles to fiction stories, and try to identify the main idea, supporting details, and any inferences you can make.

7. **Expand Your Vocabulary:** A strong vocabulary can significantly improve your comprehension skills. The more words you know, the better you'll understand what you're reading.

8. **Take Regular Practice Tests:** Regularly taking practice tests will help you become more familiar with the test format and the types of passages and questions that you'll encounter.

Remember, paragraph comprehension is a skill that improves with practice. The more you read and engage with different types of texts, the better you'll become at understanding and interpreting written information.

Practice Test with Answers

1. **Question:**

"The world's oceans are incredibly vast and deep. Because of this, a significant percentage of life on Earth exists below the ocean's surface. Despite all our

advancements in technology, we've only managed to explore a small fraction of the ocean's depths. Scientists believe that there are millions of undiscovered species living in these uncharted regions of the ocean."

Which of the following conclusions can be drawn from the paragraph?

A) Our technology is insufficient for ocean exploration.

B) Scientists are not interested in exploring the ocean.

C) There are potentially millions of undiscovered species in the ocean.

D) Life on Earth is primarily located in the ocean's depths.

Answer: C) There are potentially millions of undiscovered species in the ocean.

Explanation: The paragraph states that "Scientists believe that there are millions of undiscovered species living in these uncharted regions of the ocean," which matches answer C.

2. **Question:**

"For decades, climate scientists have been warning about the impacts of climate change. Rising global temperatures, melting ice caps, and rising sea levels are just a few of the many consequences. The changes in climate patterns also threaten biodiversity, as many species struggle to adapt to rapidly changing environments. It's clear that urgent action is needed to mitigate these impacts and protect our planet."

What is the main idea of this paragraph?

A) The melting of ice caps is the biggest concern in climate change.

B) Urgent action is needed to address the impacts of climate change.

C) Species are struggling to adapt to changing environments.

D) Rising global temperatures are causing sea levels to rise.

Answer: B) Urgent action is needed to address the impacts of climate change.

Explanation: While all the options are mentioned in the paragraph, the main idea is that urgent action is needed to address the impacts of climate change.

3. **Question:**

"Jane has always had a passion for music. Ever since she was a child, she has been playing various musical instruments and composing her own songs. Recently, she decided to turn her passion into a career by opening a music school to teach others."

Which of the following statements best summarizes the paragraph?

A) Jane recently developed a passion for music.

B) Jane has always loved music and has decided to open a music school.

C) Jane is passionate about teaching others.

D) Jane composed songs as a child.

Answer: B) Jane has always loved music and has decided to open a music school.

Explanation: The paragraph talks about Jane's lifelong passion for music and her recent decision to open a music school, which is best summarized in option B.

4. **Question:**

"Artificial intelligence (AI) is revolutionizing many industries, including healthcare. In medicine, AI can help predict disease outcomes, personalize treatment plans, and improve patient care. However, as with any technology, it's not without its challenges. Ensuring the privacy and security of patient data is one such challenge."

What is a challenge mentioned in the passage concerning the use of AI in healthcare?

A) Personalizing treatment plans

B) Predicting disease outcomes

C) Improving patient care

D) Ensuring the privacy and security of patient data

Answer: D) Ensuring the privacy and security of patient data

Explanation: The paragraph mentions that one of the challenges of using AI in healthcare is ensuring the privacy and security of patient data, which is reflected in answer D.

5. **Question:**

"Mount Everest, located in the Himalayas, is the highest peak in the world. Climbing it is a feat that many mountaineers aspire to achieve. However, the journey to the summit is dangerous and fraught with challenges such as altitude sickness, severe weather conditions, and avalanches. Despite these risks, hundreds of climbers attempt the climb each year."

What can be inferred from the paragraph about climbing Mount Everest?

A) No one should attempt to climb Mount Everest due to the risks involved.

B) Only a few mountaineers aspire to climb Mount Everest.

C) Despite the risks, many climbers attempt to climb Mount Everest each year.

D) Altitude sickness is the only risk associated with climbing Mount Everest.

Answer: C) Despite the risks, many climbers attempt to climb Mount Everest each year.

Explanation: The paragraph states that despite the risks involved, hundreds of climbers attempt the climb each year, which corresponds to answer C.

6. **Question:**

"The invention of the Internet has dramatically changed the way we communicate. Email and social media have made it possible to reach people around the world instantly. Moreover, the Internet has given everyone the ability to share their thoughts and ideas with a global audience."

What is the paragraph mainly about?

A) The benefits of social media

B) The invention of email

C) The global audience reached by Internet users

D) The impact of the Internet on communication

Answer: D) The impact of the Internet on communication

Explanation: The paragraph mainly discusses how the invention of the Internet has changed the way we communicate, corresponding to answer D.

7. **Question:**

"While solar energy is a clean and renewable source of power, it's not without its downsides. One of the biggest challenges is that solar panels only generate power when the sun is shining. This means that on cloudy days or at night, power generation is limited.

As a result, storage solutions, such as batteries, are necessary to ensure a continuous power supply."

Based on the paragraph, what is a limitation of solar energy?

A) Solar energy is not renewable.

B) Solar panels only generate power when the sun is shining.

C) Solar panels generate too much power.

D) Batteries are not suitable for storing solar energy.

Answer: B) Solar panels only generate power when the sun is shining.

Explanation: The paragraph states that one of the downsides of solar energy is that solar panels only generate power when the sun is shining, which matches answer B.

8. **Question:**

"Birds have an extraordinary ability to navigate long distances, often migrating thousands of miles each year. They use a variety of methods to navigate, including the sun, stars, and Earth's magnetic field.

This ability to find their way back to the same locations year after year is truly remarkable."

What can be inferred from the paragraph about bird navigation?

A) Birds migrate thousands of miles using GPS.

B) Birds use the sun, stars, and Earth's magnetic field for navigation.

C) Birds find it difficult to navigate long distances.

D) All birds migrate thousands of miles each year.

Answer: B) Birds use the sun, stars, and Earth's magnetic field for navigation.

Explanation: The paragraph states that birds use the sun, stars, and Earth's magnetic field for navigation, which corresponds to answer B.

9. Question:

"Water is essential for life on Earth. It makes up about 70% of the human body and is involved in numerous bodily functions. In addition to hydration, water helps with digestion, temperature regulation, and the transportation of nutrients. Without it, life as we know it would not be possible."

What is the main idea of this paragraph?

A) Water makes up 70% of the human body.

B) Water helps with digestion and temperature regulation.

C) Water is essential for life and involved in numerous bodily functions.

D) Without water, transportation of nutrients would not be possible.

Answer: C) Water is essential for life and involved in numerous bodily functions.

Explanation: While all the options are mentioned in the paragraph, the main idea is that water is essential for life and involved in numerous bodily functions, which matches answer C.

10. Question:

"Education is a critical part of personal growth and societal development. It equips individuals with knowledge and skills, fosters critical thinking, and promotes a sense of responsibility and citizenship. Through education, individuals are better prepared to face life's challenges and contribute to the development of their communities."

What can be inferred from the paragraph about education?

A) Education only promotes a sense of responsibility and citizenship.

B) Education prepares individuals to face life's challenges and contribute to their communities.

C) Only individuals who have received an education can face life's challenges.

D) Education does not foster critical thinking.

Answer: B) Education prepares individuals to face life's challenges and contribute to their communities.

Explanation: The paragraph states that through education, individuals are better prepared to face life's challenges and contribute to the development of their communities, which corresponds to answer B.

11. **Question:**

"Gardening is more than just a hobby for many people. It's a way to stay active, reduce stress, and cultivate a connection with nature. The satisfaction of growing your own fruits and vegetables can also contribute to a sense of achievement and well-being."

What is the main idea of this paragraph?

A) Gardening is a hobby for many people.

B) Gardening helps to stay active and reduce stress.

C) Growing your own fruits and vegetables contributes to well-being.

D) Gardening offers multiple benefits beyond being a mere hobby.

Answer: D) Gardening offers multiple benefits beyond being a mere hobby.

Explanation: While all options are discussed in the paragraph, the main idea is that gardening offers multiple benefits beyond being a mere hobby, which is expressed in option D.

12. **Question:**

"Computers have become an integral part of our daily lives. They are used in various fields like education, healthcare, business, and entertainment. Despite their widespread use, it's crucial to remember that they also pose certain risks. Cybersecurity threats, for instance, have become increasingly common and sophisticated."

Based on the paragraph, what is a concern related to computer use?

A) Computers are not used in healthcare.

B) Computers have become less common.

C) Cybersecurity threats have become common and sophisticated.

D) Computers are only used for entertainment purposes.

Answer: C) Cybersecurity threats have become common and sophisticated.

Explanation: The paragraph mentions that with the widespread use of computers, cybersecurity threats have become increasingly common and sophisticated, which corresponds to answer C.

13. **Question:**

"Air pollution is a significant global issue. It's caused by a variety of factors, including emissions from vehicles, industrial activities, and the burning of fossil fuels. Prolonged exposure to air pollution can lead to serious health problems like respiratory diseases, heart disease, and stroke."

What can be inferred from the paragraph about air pollution?

A) Air pollution is a minor issue.

B) Air pollution is only caused by vehicle emissions.

C) Air pollution can lead to serious health problems.

D) Industrial activities do not contribute to air pollution.

Answer: C) Air pollution can lead to serious health problems.

Explanation: The paragraph states that prolonged exposure to air pollution can lead to serious health problems, which corresponds to answer C.

14. **Question:**

"The Grand Canyon, located in Arizona, is one of the most famous natural wonders of the world. It is known for its stunning vistas and deep gorges carved by the Colorado River. Millions of visitors each year come to marvel at its beauty and scale."

What is the main idea of this paragraph?

A) The Grand Canyon is located in Arizona.

B) The Colorado River carved the Grand Canyon.

C) Millions of visitors come to the Grand Canyon each year.

D) The Grand Canyon is a famous natural wonder known for its beauty and scale.

Answer: D) The Grand Canyon is a famous natural wonder known for its beauty and scale.

Explanation: While all options are mentioned in the paragraph, the main idea is that the Grand Canyon is a famous natural wonder known for its beauty and scale, which is expressed in answer D.

15. **Question:**

_"Chocolate has been a beloved treat for centuries. It's made from the beans of the cacao tree, which are fermented, dried, and roasted to develop their characteristic flavor. The beans are then ground *into a paste called chocolate liquor, from which various types of chocolate are made. Dark chocolate, in particular, is known for its health benefits, as it contains antioxidants that can help fight off disease."*

Based on the paragraph, which type of chocolate is known for its health benefits?

A) Milk chocolate

B) White chocolate

C) Dark chocolate

D) Chocolate liquor

Answer: C) Dark chocolate

Explanation: The paragraph states that dark chocolate is known for its health benefits because it contains antioxidants that can help fight off disease. This corresponds to answer C.

15. **Question:**

"Recycling is an effective way to reduce waste and conserve natural resources. By reusing materials like paper, plastic, and metal, we can decrease the demand for new materials and reduce the energy used in production processes. It's a simple act that can have a significant impact on our environment."

What can be inferred from the paragraph about recycling?

A) Recycling is an ineffective way to reduce waste.

B) Recycling increases the demand for new materials.

C) Recycling reduces the energy used in production processes.

D) Only metal can be recycled.

Answer: C) Recycling reduces the energy used in production processes.

Explanation: The paragraph states that by recycling materials like paper, plastic, and metal, we can reduce the energy used in production processes, which corresponds to answer C.

16. **Question:**

"Regular exercise is essential for maintaining good health. It can help control weight, strengthen the heart, and improve mental health. It's recommended that adults get at least 150 minutes of moderate-intensity or 75 minutes of high-intensity exercise each week."

What is the recommended amount of exercise for adults each week, according to the paragraph?

A) 75 minutes of moderate-intensity exercise

B) 150 minutes of high-intensity exercise

C) 150 minutes of moderate-intensity or 75 minutes of high-intensity exercise

D) 300 minutes of moderate-intensity exercise

Answer: C) 150 minutes of moderate-intensity or 75 minutes of high-intensity exercise

Explanation: The paragraph states that it's recommended that adults get at least 150 minutes of moderate-intensity or 75 minutes of high-intensity exercise each week, which corresponds to answer C.

17. **Question:**

"Global warming is a serious environmental issue that poses a threat to the Earth's climate system. It's primarily caused by human activities, such as burning fossil fuels and deforestation, which increase the concentration of greenhouse gases in the atmosphere."

Based on the paragraph, what are some human activities that contribute to global warming?

A) Planting trees and recycling

B) Burning fossil fuels and deforestation

C) Conservation of water and energy

D) Eating a plant-based diet

Answer: B) Burning fossil fuels and deforestation

Explanation: The paragraph states that human activities such as burning fossil fuels and deforestation increase the concentration of greenhouse gases in the atmosphere, contributing to global warming. This corresponds to answer B.

19. Question:

"The Mona Lisa is one of the most famous paintings in the world. Painted by Leonardo da Vinci in the 16th century, it is known for the subject's enigmatic smile. The painting is housed in the Louvre Museum in Paris and is admired by millions of visitors each year."

Where is the Mona Lisa housed according to the paragraph?

A) The Louvre Museum in Paris

B) The Metropolitan Museum of Art in New York

C) The Uffizi Gallery in Florence

D) The Prado Museum in Madrid

Answer: A) The Louvre Museum in Paris

Explanation: The paragraph states that the Mona Lisa is housed in the Louvre Museum in Paris, which corresponds to answer A.

20. Question:

"Reading is a crucial skill that plays an integral role in our lives. It's not just about understanding the words on a page; it's about comprehension, critical thinking, and the ability to learn and grow from the information we consume. A lifelong love of reading can open up a world of knowledge and opportunity."

What is the main idea of this paragraph?

A) Reading is a crucial skill that plays an integral role in our lives.

B) Reading is just about understanding the words on a page.

C) A lifelong love of reading can close a world of knowledge and opportunity.

D) Comprehension and critical thinking are unrelated to reading.

Answer: A) Reading is a crucial skill that plays an integral role in our lives.

Explanation: The main idea of the paragraph is that reading is a crucial skill that plays an integral role in our lives, which corresponds to answer A.

21. **Question:**

"Solar energy is a renewable resource that has gained popularity in recent years. It involves converting sunlight into electricity using solar panels. This process is not only eco-friendly, but also cost-effective in the long run as it reduces dependency on fossil fuels."

What can be inferred from the paragraph about solar energy?

A) Solar energy is not a renewable resource.

B) Solar energy involves converting sunlight into electricity.

C) Solar energy increases dependency on fossil fuels.

D) Solar energy is not cost-effective.

Answer: B) Solar energy involves converting sunlight into electricity.

Explanation: The paragraph states that solar energy involves converting sunlight into electricity using solar panels, which corresponds to answer B.

22. **Question:**

"Public transportation is a vital part of urban living. It provides a cost-effective and environmentally friendly alternative to personal vehicles. Cities with robust *public transit systems have been found to have lower levels of air pollution and traffic congestion."*

What is the main idea of this paragraph?

A) Public transportation increases air pollution and traffic congestion.

B) Public transportation is a cost-effective and environmentally friendly alternative to personal vehicles.

C) Only cities with robust public transit systems have lower levels of air pollution.

D) Public transportation is not a part of urban living.

Answer: B) Public transportation is a cost-effective and environmentally friendly alternative to personal vehicles.

Explanation: The main idea of the paragraph is that public transportation is a cost-effective and environmentally friendly alternative to personal vehicles, which corresponds to answer B.

23. **Question:**

"The Internet has revolutionized the way we communicate and access information. It offers a wealth of resources for learning, entertainment, and social interaction. However, it also poses challenges, including privacy concerns and the spread of misinformation."

Based on the paragraph, what are some challenges posed by the Internet?

A) Privacy concerns and the spread of misinformation

B) Lack of resources for learning and entertainment

C) It has made communication more difficult

D) The Internet has reduced social interaction

Answer: A) Privacy concerns and the spread of misinformation

Explanation: The paragraph states that the Internet poses challenges, including privacy concerns and the spread of misinformation, which corresponds to answer A.

24. **Question:**

"Eating a balanced diet is important for maintaining good health. A balanced diet includes a variety of foods from all the food groups: fruits, vegetables, grains, protein foods, and dairy or dairy alternatives. It provides the nutrients our bodies need to function properly and prevent disease."

What can be inferred from the paragraph about a balanced diet?

A) A balanced diet includes only fruits and vegetables.

B) A balanced diet provides the nutrients our bodies need to function properly and prevent disease.

C) Eating a balanced diet is not important for maintaining good health.

D) A balanced diet does not include grains, protein foods, and dairy or dairy alternatives.

Answer: B) A balanced diet provides the nutrients our bodies need to function properly and prevent disease.

Explanation: The paragraph states that a balanced diet provides the nutrients our bodies need to function properly and prevent disease, which corresponds to answer B.

25. **Question:**

"Climate change is one of the most pressing issues of our time. It is largely caused by human activities that increase the concentration of greenhouse gases in the Earth's atmosphere. The consequences of climate change include rising global temperatures, melting ice caps, and more frequent extreme weather events."

What are some consequences of climate change according to the paragraph?

A) Decreasing global temperatures and increasing ice caps

B) Rising global temperatures, melting ice caps, and more frequent extreme weather events

C) Climate change is not caused by human activities

D) Climate change reduces the concentration of greenhouse gases in the Earth's atmosphere

Answer: B) Rising global temperatures, melting ice caps, and more frequent extreme weather events

Explanation: The paragraph states that the consequences of climate change include rising global temperatures, melting ice caps, and more frequent extreme weather events, which corresponds to answer B.

26. Question:

"Gardening is a rewarding hobby for many people. It can provide fresh produce, improve mental health, and even boost physical fitness. By spending time outdoors and engaging in physical activity, gardeners can enjoy the fruits of their labor and the health benefits that come with it."

According to the paragraph, what are some benefits of gardening?

A) Provides fresh produce, improves mental health, and boosts physical fitness

B) It leads to decreased physical fitness

C) Gardening cannot provide fresh produce

D) Spending time outdoors is detrimental to health

Answer: A) Provides fresh produce, improves mental health, and boosts physical fitness

Explanation: The paragraph states that gardening can provide fresh produce, improve mental health, and boost physical fitness, which corresponds to answer A.

27. Question:

"The advent of smartphones has significantly changed our day-to-day lives. These devices enable us to communicate, navigate, work, and entertain ourselves from virtually anywhere. However, excessive use can lead to negative effects such as digital addiction, sleep disturbances, and decreased social interactions."

What can be inferred from the paragraph about the excessive use of smartphones?

A) Excessive use can lead to digital addiction, sleep disturbances, and decreased social interactions

B) Excessive use increases social interactions

C) Smartphones do not allow us to communicate, navigate, work, and entertain ourselves

D) There are no negative effects of excessive smartphone use

Answer: A) Excessive use can lead to digital addiction, sleep disturbances, and decreased social interactions

Explanation: The paragraph states that excessive use of smartphones can lead to negative effects such as digital addiction, sleep disturbances, and decreased social interactions, which corresponds to answer A.

28. **Question:**

"Dogs are popular pets due to their loyal and friendly nature. They come in a wide range of breeds, each with its own unique characteristics and behaviors. Dogs can provide companionship, help reduce stress, and even serve as working animals in various roles such as guide dogs or police dogs."

What is the main idea of this paragraph?

A) Dogs are unpopular pets due to their disloyal and unfriendly nature.

B) Dogs can provide companionship, help reduce stress, and serve as working animals.

C) All dogs have the same characteristics and behaviors.

D) Dogs cannot serve as guide dogs or police dogs.

Answer: B) Dogs can provide companionship, help reduce stress, and serve as working animals.

Explanation: The main idea of the paragraph is that dogs can provide companionship, help reduce stress, and serve as working animals, which corresponds to answer B.

29. **Question:**

"Physical activity is crucial for maintaining overall health. Regular exercise can help control weight, prevent chronic diseases, improve mood and energy levels, and promote better sleep. While it's recommended to get at least 150 minutes of moderate-intensity exercise each week, even short bouts of physical activity can be beneficial."

According to the paragraph, what are some benefits of regular exercise?

A) Helps control weight, prevents chronic diseases, improves mood and energy levels, promotes better sleep

B) Leads to weight gain and chronic diseases

C) Decreases mood and energy levels, leads to poor sleep

D) Physical activity is not beneficial

Answer: A) Helps control weight, prevents chronic diseases, improves mood and energy levels, promotes better sleep

Explanation: The paragraph states that regular exercise can help control weight, prevent chronic diseases, improve mood and energy levels, and promote better sleep, which corresponds to answer A.

30. Question:

"Music is a universal form of expression. It has the power to evoke emotions, convey messages, and bring people together. From classical to rock, jazz to pop, music spans a wide range of genres and styles. Regardless of personal preferences, music plays a significant role in cultures around the world."

What can be inferred from the paragraph about music?

A) Music is a universal form of expression that can evoke emotions, convey messages, and bring people together

B) Music is not a form of expression and cannot evoke emotions or convey messages

C) Only classical music plays a significant role in cultures around the world

D) Personal preferences do not play a role in the appreciation of music

Answer: A) Music is a universal form of expression that can evoke emotions, convey messages, and bring people together

Explanation: The paragraph states that music is a universal form of expression that can evoke emotions, convey messages, and bring people together, which corresponds to answer A.

31. **Question:**

"Volunteering offers numerous benefits both for individuals and the community. It can help people gain new skills and experiences, expand their network, and foster a sense of achievement. At the same time, it also contributes to social causes and community development."

What are some benefits of volunteering according to the paragraph?

A) Volunteering can lead to loss of skills and experiences.

B) Volunteering has no impact on social causes and community development.

C) Volunteering helps people gain new skills and experiences, expand their network, and fosters a sense of achievement.

D) Volunteering limits an individual's network.

Answer: C) Volunteering helps people gain new skills and experiences, expand their network, and fosters a sense of achievement.

Explanation: The paragraph indicates that volunteering can help individuals gain new skills and experiences, expand their network, and foster a sense of achievement, which aligns with answer C.

32. **Question:**

"Coffee is one of the most popular beverages worldwide. It's enjoyed for its rich flavor and stimulating effect, largely due to its caffeine content. However, excessive consumption can lead to side effects like insomnia, restlessness, and an upset stomach."

What can be inferred from the paragraph about excessive coffee consumption?

A) Excessive consumption can lead to insomnia, restlessness, and an upset stomach.

B) Coffee is unpopular worldwide.

C) Excessive consumption of coffee has no side effects.

D) The caffeine content in coffee has a calming effect.

Answer: A) Excessive consumption can lead to insomnia, restlessness, and an upset stomach.

Explanation: The paragraph mentions that excessive coffee consumption can lead to side effects like insomnia, restlessness, and an upset stomach, corresponding to answer A.

33. **Question:**

"Recycling is a key part of waste management strategies worldwide. It involves converting waste materials into reusable materials, reducing the demand for new raw materials and the amount of waste that ends up in landfills. Not only is it beneficial for the environment, but it can also be economically advantageous."

What is the main idea of this paragraph?

A) Recycling involves converting waste materials into reusable materials and is beneficial for the environment and economy.

B) Recycling increases the demand for new raw materials.

C) Recycling contributes to the amount of waste in landfills.

D) Recycling has no economic advantages.

Answer: A) Recycling involves converting waste materials into reusable materials and is beneficial for the environment and economy.

Explanation: The main idea of the paragraph is that recycling involves converting waste materials into reusable materials and is beneficial for both the environment and the economy, aligning with answer A.

34. **Question:**

"The Grand Canyon, located in the U.S. state of Arizona, is a natural wonder known for its impressive size and colorful landscape. Formed by millions of years of erosion by the Colorado River, it's a popular destination for tourists and outdoor enthusiasts."

What can be inferred from the paragraph about the Grand Canyon?

A) The Grand Canyon is a man-made structure in Arizona.

B) The Grand Canyon was formed by millions of years of erosion by the Colorado River.

C) The Grand Canyon is unpopular among tourists and outdoor enthusiasts.

D) The Grand Canyon is known for its limited size and monotone landscape.

Answer: B) The Grand Canyon was formed by millions of years of erosion by the Colorado River.

Explanation: The paragraph states that the Grand Canyon was formed by millions of years of erosion by the Colorado River, which matches with answer B.

35. **Question:**

"Exercise and a balanced diet are essential for maintaining a healthy lifestyle. Regular physical activity can help maintain a healthy weight and reduce the risk of various diseases, while a balanced diet provides the necessary nutrients for overall wellbeing."

What are some benefits of exercise and a balanced diet according to the paragraph?

A) Exercise and a balanced diet can lead to an unhealthy lifestyle.

B) Exercise can help maintain a healthy weight and reduce the risk of various diseases, while a balanced diet provides the necessary nutrients for overall wellbeing.

C) Regular physical activity increases the risk of various diseases.

D) A balanced diet provides unnecessary nutrients for overall wellbeing.

Answer: B) Exercise can help maintain a healthy weight and reduce the risk of various diseases, while a balanced diet provides the necessary nutrients for overall wellbeing.

Explanation: The paragraph states that regular physical activity can help maintain a healthy weight and reduce the risk of various diseases, and a balanced diet provides the necessary nutrients for overall wellbeing, which corresponds to answer B.

36. **Question:**

"Reading books is a hobby cherished by many. It not only provides a source of entertainment but also enhances knowledge and stimulates the mind. Different genres like fiction, non-fiction, fantasy, and biographies cater to diverse tastes and preferences of readers."

What can be inferred from the paragraph about reading books?

A) Reading books is a source of entertainment, enhances knowledge, and stimulates the mind.

B) Reading books is disliked by many.

C) Reading books provides no enhancement to knowledge or mental stimulation.

D) All readers have the same taste and preference in book genres.

Answer: A) Reading books is a source of entertainment, enhances knowledge, and stimulates the mind.

Explanation: The paragraph states that reading books provides entertainment, enhances knowledge, and stimulates the mind, which aligns with answer A.

37. **Question:**

"Photography is an art form that captures moments in time. It allows people to express their creativity, preserve memories, and communicate ideas. Whether it's through portrait, landscape, or abstract photography, each image tells a story."

What is the main idea of this paragraph?

A) Photography captures moments in time and allows people to express creativity, preserve memories, and communicate ideas.

B) Photography does not allow people to express their creativity.

C) All types of photography tell the same story.

D) Photography does not preserve memories or communicate ideas.

Answer: A) Photography captures moments in time and allows people to express creativity, preserve memories, and communicate ideas.

Explanation: The main idea of the paragraph is that photography captures moments in time and allows people to express their creativity, preserve memories, and communicate ideas, which aligns with answer A.

38. **Question:**

"Solar energy is a renewable and clean form of energy. It harnesses the power of the sun to generate electricity, reducing reliance on fossil fuels. As technology advances, solar energy is becoming more accessible and affordable, promoting sustainable development."

What can be inferred from the paragraph about solar energy?

A) Solar energy is a non-renewable and polluting form of energy.

B) Solar energy harnesses the power of the sun to generate electricity and promotes sustainable development.

C) Solar energy increases reliance on fossil fuels.

D) Advances in technology make solar energy less accessible and affordable.

Answer: B) Solar energy harnesses the power of the sun to generate electricity and promotes sustainable development.

Explanation: The paragraph states that solar energy harnesses the power of the sun to generate electricity and promotes sustainable development, which corresponds to answer B.

39. **Question:**

"Yoga is an ancient practice that combines physical postures, breathing exercises, and meditation. It enhances flexibility, strength, and balance, while promoting mindfulness and stress relief. With its roots in India, yoga has gained worldwide popularity due to its physical and mental health benefits."

According to the paragraph, what are some benefits of yoga?

A) Enhances flexibility, strength, and balance, promotes mindfulness and stress relief.

B) Yoga reduces flexibility, strength, and balance.

C) Yoga has no roots in India and is not popular worldwide.

D) Yoga does not offer any physical or mental health benefits.

Answer: A) Enhances flexibility, strength, and balance, promotes mindfulness and stress relief.

Explanation: The paragraph states that yoga enhances flexibility, strength, and balance, while promoting mindfulness and stress relief, which corresponds to answer A.

40. **Question:**

"Volcanoes are fascinating natural phenomena that result from the movement of tectonic plates in the Earth's crust. While they can be destructive due to eruptions, they also contribute to land formation and nutrient-rich soil."

What can be inferred from the paragraph about volcanoes?

A) Volcanoes are man-made phenomena that result from human activity.

B) Volcanoes can be destructive due to eruptions, but they also contribute to land formation and nutrient-rich soil.

C) Volcanoes prevent the movement of tectonic plates in the Earth's crust.

D) Volcanoes contribute to land degradation and nutrient-poor soil.

Answer: B) Volcanoes can be destructive due to eruptions, but they also contribute to land formation and nutrient-rich soil.

Explanation: The paragraph states that volcanoes can be destructive due to eruptions, but they also contribute to land formation and nutrient-rich soil, which aligns with answer B.

Paragraph Comprehension Test Strategies

Paragraph Comprehension is a vital part of the ASVAB test, and having a solid strategy can significantly increase your chances of scoring high. Here are some key strategies to use:

1. Understand the Structure of Paragraphs:

Paragraphs generally follow a structure: introduction, body, and conclusion. The introductory sentence usually introduces the main idea or topic. The body provides additional information and details about the topic. The concluding sentence wraps up the paragraph, sometimes summarizing or providing a final thought on the topic. Understanding this structure can help you determine the main idea and important details of a paragraph.

2. Skim the Questions Before Reading:

Before diving into the passage, skim through the questions. This will give you an idea of the information you should be looking for when reading. It saves time and helps you focus on the key points in the paragraph.

3. Take Short Notes:

While reading the passage, jot down short notes about the main idea and crucial details. This will save you from going back and forth between the questions and the passage.

4. Draw Inferences:

Some questions require you to make inferences or draw conclusions based on the information provided in the paragraph. This requires you to read "between the lines." Practice this skill to get a deeper understanding of the text.

5. Be Aware of Transition Words:

Words such as however, therefore, and nevertheless, often signal a change or addition to the author's thought. These words can significantly help in understanding the meaning of the paragraph.

6. Be Mindful of the Time:

The ASVAB is a timed test, so efficient use of time is crucial. Avoid spending too much time on one question. If you find a question difficult, move on to the next and return to it later if time allows.

7. Practice:

Lastly, like any other test, practice is key. Utilize practice tests to get a feel for the types of questions you'll encounter. This will also help you understand your strengths and areas where you need improvement.

Remember, these strategies may take time to master, so start preparing early. Good luck with your ASVAB test preparation!

Chapter 6
Mathematics Knowledge

Overview and Study Guide

The Mathematics Knowledge section of the ASVAB test is designed to evaluate your understanding of high school level mathematics. This includes topics like algebra, geometry, and basic arithmetic. It's not just about knowing the concepts, but also about applying them to solve problems. The questions in this section are often framed in real-world scenarios that require you to use mathematical principles to find solutions.

The Mathematics Knowledge section carries a significant weight in the computation of your AFQT (Armed Forces Qualifying Test) score, which determines your eligibility for enlistment in the Navy. Therefore, a good performance in this section can greatly enhance your overall ASVAB score.

Study Guide

Here are some of the main topics that you should focus on while preparing for the Mathematics Knowledge section:

1. **Arithmetic Operations:** You should be comfortable with basic operations including addition, subtraction, multiplication, and division. This also includes understanding of fractions, decimals, and percentages.

2. **Algebra:** This includes solving simple and complex equations, factoring, understanding the concept of variables, and applying the laws of exponents. Knowledge of both linear and quadratic equations can be beneficial.

3. **Geometry:** This area covers concepts such as calculating area, volume, and perimeter of various geometric shapes. Understanding angles, triangles, circles, and the Pythagorean theorem is also important.

4. **Word Problems:** You should be able to translate word problems into mathematical equations and solve them. These can involve various topics, such as rate, time and distance problems, age problems, and mixture problems.

5. **Number Theory:** Basic understanding of prime numbers, multiples, and factors, as well as the principles of divisibility, can also be part of the test.

To prepare effectively for the Mathematics Knowledge section, begin by assessing your current skill level. Identify areas where you need more practice and focus on those. Review mathematical concepts and practice applying them in different contexts. Use flashcards to remember formulas and concepts. Also, practice under timed conditions to get a feel for the pace of the test.

Lastly, remember to use the practice tests and questions provided in this book. They will help familiarize you with the format of the questions and will give you a good idea of what to expect in the actual test. Good luck with your preparation!

Practice Test with Answers

1. Question:

If $x = 2$ and $y = 3$, what is the value of $4x^2 - 3y$?

A) 2 B) 7 C) 5 D) 8

Answer: B) 7

Explanation: Substitute $x = 2$ and $y = 3$ into the equation. We get $4(2)^2 - 3(3) = 16 - 9 = 7$.

2. Question:

What is the area of a rectangle with a length of 5 units and a width of 3 units?

A) 15 square units B) 16 square units C) 8 square units D) 12 square units

Answer: A) 15 square units

Explanation: The area of a rectangle is calculated as length x width = 5 units x 3 units = 15 square units.

3. Question:

Solve for x: 4x - 2 = 18

A) 6 B) 5 C) 7 D) 4

Answer: A) 6

Explanation: Add 2 to both sides of the equation to get 4x = 20, then divide both sides by 4 to solve for x, resulting in x = 6.

4. Question:

If a square has a side length of 7 units, what is its perimeter?

A) 28 units B) 14 units C) 21 units D) 35 units

Answer: A) 28 units

Explanation: The perimeter of a square is calculated by multiplying the length of one side by 4. Therefore, 7 units x 4 = 28 units.

5. Question:

What is the value of 7^3?

A) 343 B) 21 C) 49 D) 210

Answer: A) 343

Explanation: The cube of a number (n^3) is the number multiplied by itself twice. So, 7^3 = 7 x 7 x 7 = 343.

6. Question:

If the radius of a circle is 3 units, what is the area of the circle? (Use 3.14 for π)

A) 28.26 square units B) 18.84 square units C) 9.42 square units D) 37.68 square units

Answer: A) 28.26 square units

Explanation: The area of a circle is $πr^2$. Substituting the given values, we get 3.14 x $(3)^2$ = 3.14 x 9 = 28.26 square units.

7. Question:

Simplify the expression: 5(3x - 2)

A) 15x - 2 B) 15x - 10 C) 8x - 2 D) 8x - 10

Answer: B) 15x - 10

Explanation: Apply the distributive property 5 * 3x - 5 * 2 = 15x - 10.

8. Question:

Solve for x: 3x + 5 = 14

A) 1 B) 2 C) 3 D) 4

Answer: C) 3

Explanation: Subtract 5 from both sides of the equation to get 3x = 9, then divide both sides by 3 to solve for x, giving x = 3.

9. Question:

What is the greatest common factor of 36 and 54?

A) 6 B) 9 C) 18 D) 36

Answer: C) 18

Explanation: The factors of 36 are 1, 2, 3, 4, 6, 9, 12, 18, and 36. The factors of 54 are 1, 2, 3, 6, 9, 18, 27, and 54. The greatest number that appears in both lists is 18.

10. Question:

What is the result when you multiply a number by its reciprocal?

A) 0 B) 1 C) The original number D) Undefined

Answer: B) 1

Explanation: A number multiplied by its reciprocal always equals 1. For example, the reciprocal of 4 is 1/4, and 4 * 1/4 = 1.

11. Question:

In a right triangle, if one of the angles measures 45 degrees, what is the measure of the other non-right angle?

A) 30 degrees B) 45 degrees C) 60 degrees D) 90 degrees

Answer: B) 45 degrees

Explanation: In a right triangle, the sum of the measures of the three angles is 180 degrees. If one angle is 90 degrees (right angle) and the other is 45 degrees, the remaining angle must also be 45 degrees (because 180 - 90 - 45 = 45).

12. Question:

What is the value of 2x - 3 when x equals 5?

A) 4 B) 7 C) 9 D) 10

Answer: B) 7

Explanation: Replace x with 5 in the expression to get 2(5) - 3 = 10 - 3 = 7.

13. Question:

What is the sum of the interior angles of a pentagon?

A) 360 degrees B) 540 degrees C) 720 degrees D) 900 degrees

Answer: B) 540 degrees

Explanation: The sum of the interior angles of any polygon is given by the formula (n-2)*180, where n is the number of sides. A pentagon has 5 sides, so its interior angles sum to (5-2) *180 = 540 degrees.

14. Question:

If the price of a shirt is reduced by 20% to sell for $48, what was the original price?

A) $60 B) $58 C) $56 D) $54

Answer: A) $60

Explanation: The discounted price is 80% of the original price (since 100% - 20% = 80%). So, $48 is

80% of the original price. To find the original price, divide $48 by 0.8 to get $60.

15. Question:

Solve for x: 5(x - 3) = 2(x + 5)

A) 5 B) 4 C) 3 D) 2

Answer: A) 5

Explanation: Apply the distributive property to get 5x - 15 = 2x + 10. Subtract 2x from both sides to get 3x - 15 = 10. Add 15 to both sides to get 3x = 25. Divide both sides by 3 to get x = 5.

16. Question:

What is the area of a circle with a diameter of 10 units? (Use 3.14 for π)

A) 31.4 square units B) 78.5 square units C) 314 square units D) 100 square units

Answer: C) 314 square units

Explanation: The area of a circle is πr^2. The radius is half of the diameter, so for a circle with a diameter of 10 units, the radius is 5 units. Substituting the given values, we get 3.14 x (5)² = 3.14 x 25 = 78.5 square units.

17. Question:

If y = 3x + 5 and x = 4, what is the value of y?

A) 12 B) 17 C) 21 D) 25

Answer: B) 17

Explanation: Replace x with 4 in the equation to get y = 3(4) + 5 = 12 + 5 = 17.

18. Question:

A car travels at a constant speed of 60 miles per hour. How far does it travel in 2.5 hours?

A) 120 miles B) 150 miles C) 180 miles D) 210 miles

Answer: B) 150 miles

Explanation: Distance is equal to speed times time. So, 60 miles per hour x 2.5 hours = 150 miles.

19. Question:

What is the volume of a cube with side length of 4 units?

A) 16 cubic units B) 32 cubic units C) 48 cubic units D) 64 cubic units

Answer: D) 64 cubic units

Explanation: The volume of a cube is calculated by cubing the length of one side. Therefore, 4 units³ = 64 cubic units.

20. Question:

What is the solution to the equation 2x - 5 = 3x + 2?

A) -7 B) -3 C) 3 D) 7

Answer: A) -7

Explanation: Subtract 2x from both sides to get -5 = x + 2. Then, subtract 2 from both sides to get x = -7.

21. Question:

Simplify the expression: 12x + 4y - 3x + 2y

A) 15x + 6y B) 9x + 6y C) 9x + 2y D) 15x + 2y

Answer: B) 9x + 6y

Explanation: Combine like terms to simplify the expression: 12x - 3x + 4y + 2y = 9x + 6y.

22. Question:

If y = 2x - 3 and x = -1, what is the value of y?

A) -1 B) -2 C) -3 D) -5

Answer: D) -5

Explanation: Substitute x = -1 into the equation, we get y = 2(-1) - 3 = -2 - 3 = -5.

23. Question:

What is the sum of the first 50 positive integers?

A) 1275 B) 1250 C) 1300 D) 1325

Answer: A) 1275

Explanation: The sum of the first n positive integers is given by the formula n(n+1)/2. So, the sum of the first 50 positive integers is 50(50 + 1) / 2 = 50(51) / 2 = 1275.

24. Question:

What is the midpoint of the line segment with endpoints (-4, 2) and (4, 6)?

A) (0, 4) B) (-2, 3) C) (2, 4) D) (0, 3)

Answer: A) (0, 4)

Explanation: The midpoint of a line segment with endpoints (x_1, y_1) and (x_2, y_2) is given by $((x_1 + x_2) / 2, (y_1 + y_2) / 2)$. So, the midpoint of the line segment with endpoints (-4, 2) and (4, 6) is ((-4 + 4) / 2, (2 + 6) / 2) = (0, 4).

25. Question:

If 3x - 2y = 12 and y = 2, what is the value of x?

A) 4 B) 5 C) 6 D) 8

Answer: A) 4

Explanation: Substitute y = 2 into the equation to get 3x - 2(2) = 12, or 3x - 4 = 12. Add 4 to both sides to get 3x = 16. Divide both sides by 3 to get x = 16/3, which simplifies to approximately x = 4.

26. Question:

What is the value of $\sqrt{49}$?

A) 5 B) 6 C) 7 D) 8

Answer: C) 7

Explanation: The square root of 49 is 7, because 7^2 = 49.

27. Question:

What is the perimeter of a rectangle with a length of 7 units and a width of 3 units?

A) 14 units B) 20 units C) 24 units D) 28 units

Answer: B) 20 units

Explanation: The perimeter of a rectangle is 2(length + width). So, 2(7 + 3) = 2(10) = 20 units.

28. Question:

If a train travels 360 miles in 3 hours, what is its average speed in miles per hour?

A) 90 mph B) 120 mph C) 180 mph D) 240 mph

Answer: B) 120 mph

Explanation: Average speed is total distance divided by total time. So, 360 miles divided by 3 hours equals 120 miles per hour.

29. Question:

Solve for y: 3y - 2 = 7

A) 1 B) 2 C) 3 D) 4

Answer: C) 3

Explanation: Add 2 to both sides of the equation to get 3y = 9. Then, divide both sides by 3 to get y = 3.

30. Question:

What is the slope of a line that passes through the points (2, 3) and (4, 7)?

A) 1 B) 2 C) 3 D) 4

Answer: B) 2

Explanation: The slope of a line through points (x_1, y_1) and (x_2, y_2) is given by $(y_2 - y_1) / (x_2 - x_1)$. So, the slope of the line through (2, 3) and (4, 7) is $(7 - 3) / (4 - 2) = 4 / 2 = 2$.

31. Question:

What is the area of a triangle with a base of 10 units and a height of 5 units?

A) 25 sq units B) 50 sq units C) 100 sq units D) 200 sq units

Answer: B) 50 sq units

Explanation: The area of a triangle is given by (base x height)/2. So, the area of the triangle is (10 x 5)/2 = 50 square units.

32. Question:

Simplify the expression: 5(2x - 3) - 4x

A) 2x - 15 B) 6x - 15 C) 10x - 15 D) 10x - 12

Answer: B) 6x - 15

Explanation: Distribute the 5 across (2x - 3) to get 10x - 15. Then subtract 4x to get 6x - 15.

33. Question:

If a car travels at 50 miles per hour for 2.5 hours, how far does it travel?

A) 75 miles B) 100 miles C) 125 miles D) 150 miles

Answer: C) 125 miles

Explanation: Distance is equal to speed times time. So, 50 miles per hour x 2.5 hours = 125 miles.

34. Question:

Solve for x: 5x - 3 = 17

A) 2 B) 3 C) 4 D) 5

Answer: C) 4

Explanation: Add 3 to both sides of the equation to get 5x = 20. Then, divide both sides by 5 to get x = 4.

35. Question:

What is the volume of a rectangular prism with a length of 4 units, a width of 3 units, and a height of 2 units?

A) 12 cubic units B) 24 cubic units C) 36 cubic units D) 48 cubic units

Answer: B) 24 cubic units

Explanation: The volume of a rectangular prism is length x width x height. So, the volume of this prism is 4 units x 3 units x 2 units = 24 cubic units.

36. Question:

If the perimeter of a square is 20 units, what is the length of each side?

A) 2.5 units B) 5 units C) 10 units D) 20 units

Answer: B) 5 units

Explanation: The perimeter of a square is 4 times the length of one side. So, 20 units divided by 4 = 5 units per side.

37. Question:

What is the solution to the equation 3x + 2 = 14?

A) 2 B) 3 C) 4 D) 5

Answer: D) 5

Explanation: Subtract 2 from both sides to get 3x = 12. Then, divide both sides by 3 to get x = 5.

38. Question:

If a rectangle has a perimeter of 24 units and the length is 7 units, what is the width?

A) 2 units B) 3 units C) 4 units D) 5 units

Answer: D) 5 units

Explanation: The perimeter of a rectangle is given by the formula 2(length + width). So, 24 = 2(7 + width), 24 = 14 + 2width, 10 = 2width, and thus width = 5 units.

39. Question:

If a triangle has sides of 3, 4, and 5 units, is it a right triangle?

A) Yes B) No

Answer: A) Yes

Explanation: If a triangle with sides of length a, b, and c (where c is the longest side) is a right triangle, it will satisfy the Pythagorean theorem $a^2 + b^2 = c^2$. For this triangle, $3^2 + 4^2 = 9 + 16 = 25$, which is indeed equal to 5^2. So, this is a right triangle.

40. Question:

Solve the following equation for y: 2y + 3 = 9

A) 1 B) 2 C) 3 D) 4

Answer: C) 3

Explanation: Subtract 3 from both sides of the equation to get 2y = 6. Then divide both sides by 2 to find y = 3.

41. Question:

Convert the fraction 7/8 to a decimal.

A) 0.75 B) 0.875 C) 0.78 D) 0.88

Answer: B) 0.875

Explanation: To convert the fraction 7/8 to a decimal, divide the numerator by the denominator to get 0.875.

42. Question:

If x = 2 and y = 3, what is the value of the expression $2x^2 - 3y$?

A) -1 B) 1 C) 5 D) 7

Answer: B) 1

Explanation: Substitute x = 2 and y = 3 into the expression to get $2(2)^2 - 3(3) = 2(4) - 9 = 8 - 9 = -1$.

43. Question:

Simplify the expression: 6x + 5 - 2x + 3

A) 4x + 8 B) 4x + 2 C) 8x + 8 D) 8x + 2

Answer: A) 4x + 8

Explanation: Combine like terms to simplify the expression: 6x - 2x + 5 + 3 = 4x + 8.

44. Question:

If a circle has a radius of 7 units, what is its area?

A) 49π sq units B) 28π sq units C) 21π sq units D) 14π sq units

Answer: A) 49π sq units

Explanation: The area of a circle is given by the formula π(radius²). So, the area of the circle is π(7^2) = 49π square units.

45. Question:

What is the value of $\sqrt{81}$?

A) 6 B) 7 C) 8 D) 9

Answer: D) 9

Explanation: The square root of 81 is 9, since 9*9 = 81.

46. Question:

What is the median of the following set of numbers: 7, 12, 3, 9, 10?

A) 7 B) 9 C) 10 D) 12

Answer: B) 9

Explanation: To find the median, we first need to put the numbers in order from smallest to largest: 3, 7, 9, 10, 12. The median is the middle number, which in this case is 9.

47. Question:

If a cube has a side length of 3 units, what is its volume?

A) 9 cubic units B) 18 cubic units C) 27 cubic units D) 36 cubic units

Answer: C) 27 cubic units

Explanation: The volume of a cube is found by cubing the side length, so $3^3 = 27$ cubic units.

48. Question:

Solve for x: 4x - 10 = 14

A) 3 B) 4 C) 5 D) 6

Answer: D) 6

Explanation: First, add 10 to both sides of the equation to get 4x = 24. Then, divide both sides by 4 to get x = 6.

49. Question:

If a rectangle has an area of 72 square units and a length of 9 units, what is the width?

A) 5 units B) 6 units C) 7 units D) 8 units

Answer: D) 8 units

Explanation: The area of a rectangle is given by the formula length x width. So, to find the width, we can divide the area by the length: 72 ÷ 9 = 8 units.

50. Question:

What is the slope of a line that passes through the points (2, 4) and (6, 10)?

A) 1 B) 1.5 C) 2 D) 2.5

Answer: C) 2

Explanation: The slope of a line through points (x_1, y_1) and (x_2, y_2) is given by $(y_2 - y_1) / (x_2 - x_1)$. So, the slope of the line through (2, 4) and (6, 10) is (10 - 4) / (6 - 2) = 6 / 4 = 1.5.

Mathematics Knowledge Test Strategies

1. **Review and Understand Basic Mathematical Concepts:** Before taking the ASVAB, it's important to have a solid understanding of basic mathematical concepts, including algebra,

geometry, and basic arithmetic. These concepts form the foundation of the Mathematics Knowledge subtest. If you find that you're struggling with a certain area, take the time to review it thoroughly.

2. **Practice Problem Solving:** The Mathematics Knowledge subtest isn't just about knowing mathematical concepts—it's also about being able to apply them to solve problems. Practice problem-solving regularly to become comfortable with applying your mathematical knowledge.

3. **Brush Up on Your Formula Knowledge:** The Mathematics Knowledge subtest will test your ability to recall and use a variety of mathematical formulas. For example, you'll need to remember the formulas for calculating the area and perimeter of different shapes, the Pythagorean theorem, and the formula for calculating the volume of a cube or cylinder.

4. **Use Estimation:** When you're unsure of an answer, estimation can often help you eliminate incorrect answer choices. For example, if the question is asking for the product of 25 and 16,

you know that the answer must be more than 400 but less than 500. This can help you narrow down your choices.

5. **Watch Your Time:** You'll only have a certain amount of time to complete the Mathematics Knowledge subtest, so it's important to watch your time. Don't spend too much time on any single question. If you find that you're stuck, it may be better to make an educated guess and move on.

6. **Practice, Practice, Practice:** Lastly, but most importantly, practice as much as possible. Use ASVAB practice tests to become familiar with the types of questions you'll be asked, and to assess your strengths and weaknesses. The more you practice, the more comfortable you'll become with the test format and the types of questions you'll encounter.

Remember, success on the ASVAB is all about preparation. If you understand the basic concepts, remember the formulas, and practice your problem-solving skills, you'll have a strong foundation for success on the Mathematics Knowledge subtest.

Chapter 7
Electronics Information

Overview and Study Guide

The Electronics Information (EI) subtest of the ASVAB measures your knowledge of electrical equipment and parts, including circuits, currents, batteries, and electrical symbols. This test will also assess your understanding of the principles of electric power, the operation of electronic devices, and the use of tools to measure and perform work on electronic devices.

Here are some of the key concepts you'll need to understand for this section:

1. **Electricity Basics:** This includes understanding the difference between alternating current (AC) and direct current (DC), how to calculate voltage, current, and resistance using Ohm's Law (V=IR), and the functions of series and parallel circuits.

2. **Electrical Components:** You'll need to be familiar with common electronic components, including resistors, capacitors, inductors, transformers, and transistors. Understanding what each component

does and how it impacts a circuit or system is crucial.

3. **Schematic Diagrams:** The test will include questions that require you to read and interpret schematic diagrams. These diagrams use standardized symbols to represent electrical and electronic devices.

4. **Power Systems:** This section includes understanding the concepts of electrical power and energy, as well as the power ratings of different electrical devices.

5. **Electronic Devices:** Understanding how various electronic devices work, including radios, televisions, and other household appliances will be tested.

6. **Tools and Measurements:** Finally, you should be familiar with the tools used for electronic repair and maintenance, as well as the units of measurement used in electronics.

To study for this subtest, start by reviewing the basics of electrical theory and circuit analysis. Understand the function of each electronic component and how they work together in a circuit. Practice reading and interpreting schematic diagrams. Finally, familiarize yourself with the common electronic devices and tools. There are many resources available online, including tutorial videos and practice questions that can help you get a better understanding of these topics.

Practice Test with Answers

1. Question:

What is the symbol for a resistor in a schematic diagram?

A) A zigzag line B) A straight line C) A circle D) A square

Answer: A) A zigzag line

Explanation: In a schematic diagram, a resistor is represented by a zigzag line.

2. Question:

Which electronic component stores electrical energy in an electrostatic field?

A) Resistor B) Inductor C) Capacitor D) Transistor

Answer: C) Capacitor

Explanation: A capacitor is an electronic component that stores electrical energy in an electrostatic field.

3. Question:

Which tool would be used to measure the current in an electronic circuit?

A) Voltmeter B) Ohmmeter C) Ammeter D) Multimeter

Answer: C) Ammeter

Explanation: An ammeter is used to measure current in a circuit.

4. Question:

What is the primary function of a transformer in an electronic circuit?

A) To resist current flow B) To amplify signals C) To store energy D) To change the voltage level

Answer: D) To change the voltage level

Explanation: The primary function of a transformer in an electronic circuit is to change the voltage level.

5. Question:

What is the unit of measurement for electrical resistance?

A) Ampere B) Ohm C) Volt D) Watt

Answer: B) Ohm

Explanation: The ohm is the unit of measurement for electrical resistance.

6. Question:

In a series circuit with a 10-ohm, a 20-ohm, and a 30-ohm resistor, what is the total resistance?

A) 30 ohms B) 60 ohms C) 90 ohms D) 120 ohms

Answer: B) 60 ohms

Explanation: In a series circuit, the total resistance is the sum of the individual resistances.

7. Question:

What is the formula for Ohm's Law?

A) I = V/R B) V = I/R C) R = V/I D) V = I*R

Answer: D) V = I*R

Explanation: Ohm's Law states that the voltage (V) across a resistor is the product of the current (I) and the resistance (R).

8. Question:

What type of current does a battery produce?

A) Alternating current B) Direct current C) Induced current D) Polarized current

Answer: B) Direct current

Explanation: A battery produces direct current, which flows in one direction.

9. Question:

What electronic component can amplify signals?

A) Resistor B) Capacitor C) Transistor D) Inductor

Answer: C) Transistor

Explanation: A transistor can amplify signals in an electronic circuit.

10. Question:

Which of the following is a semiconductor device?

A) Capacitor B) Inductor C) Resistor D) Diode

Answer: D) Diode

Explanation: A diode is a semiconductor device that allows current to flow in one direction only.

11. Question:

What is the unit of capacitance?

A) Ohm B) Farad C) Ampere D) Henry

Answer: B) Farad

Explanation: The unit of capacitance is the Farad, named after Michael Faraday.

12. Question:

What type of circuit allows current to take multiple paths?

A) Series circuit B) Parallel circuit C) Short circuit D) Open circuit

Answer: B) Parallel circuit

Explanation: In a parallel circuit, the electric current has multiple paths to follow.

13. Question:

Which tool is used to measure the resistance of a component?

A) Ammeter B) Voltmeter C) Oscilloscope D) Ohmmeter

Answer: D) Ohmmeter

Explanation: An ohmmeter is used to measure the resistance of a component in a circuit.

14. Question:

What does an inductor primarily do in a circuit?

A) Stores electric charge B) Resists the flow of current C) Stores energy in a magnetic field D) Changes the voltage level

Answer: C) Stores energy in a magnetic field

Explanation: An inductor primarily stores energy in a magnetic field when electric current flows through it.

15. Question:

What device is used to transform AC to DC?

A) Transformer B) Resistor C) Capacitor D) Rectifier

Answer: D) Rectifier

Explanation: A rectifier is an electrical device that converts alternating current (AC), which periodically reverses direction, to direct current (DC), which flows in only one direction.

16. Question:

What type of electronic component is used to limit the amount of current in a circuit?

A) Diode B) Transistor C) Resistor D) Capacitor

Answer: C) Resistor

Explanation: A resistor is an electronic component that is used to limit the amount of current in a circuit.

17. Question:

Which of the following is not a type of transistor?

A) Bipolar junction transistor (BJT) B) Field-effect transistor (FET) C) Junction gate field-effect transistor (JFET) D) Rectifier

Answer: D) Rectifier

Explanation: A rectifier is not a type of transistor. It is a device that converts alternating current (AC) to direct current (DC).

18. Question:

What is the process of increasing the strength of a signal called?

A) Rectification B) Oscillation C) Amplification D) Modulation

Answer: C) Amplification

Explanation: Amplification is the process of increasing the strength of a signal.

19. Question:

What is the symbol for a battery in a schematic diagram?

A) A series of parallel lines with alternate lines being shorter B) A circle with a cross inside C) A straight line D) A zigzag line

Answer: A) A series of parallel lines with alternate lines being shorter

Explanation: In a schematic diagram, a battery is usually represented by a series of parallel lines with alternate lines being shorter.

20. Question:

What is the principle that states that the current through a conductor between two points is directly proportional to the voltage across the two points?

A) Faraday's Law B) Ohm's Law C) Coulomb's Law D) Kirchhoff's Law

Answer: B) Ohm's Law

Explanation: Ohm's Law states that the current through a conductor between two points is directly proportional to the voltage across the two points.

21. Question:

What device is used to measure voltage in a circuit?

A) Ohmmeter B) Ammeter C) Voltmeter D) Multimeter

Answer: C) Voltmeter

Explanation: A voltmeter is used to measure the voltage across two points in an electronic circuit.

22. Question:

In terms of electricity, what does AC stand for?

A) Automatic Conversion B) Alternating Current C) Amplitude Compression D) Absolute Capacitance

Answer: B) Alternating Current

Explanation: AC stands for Alternating Current, a type of electrical current where the flow of electric charge periodically reverses direction.

23. Question:

What component is typically used to store charge in an electronic circuit?

A) Resistor B) Inductor C) Capacitor D) Diode

Answer: C) Capacitor

Explanation: A capacitor is typically used to store charge in an electronic circuit.

24. Question:

In a closed electrical circuit, what will an increase in resistance cause?

A) An increase in current B) A decrease in current C) No change in current D) A short circuit

Answer: B) A decrease in current

Explanation: According to Ohm's Law, in a closed electrical circuit, an increase in resistance will cause a decrease in current.

25. Question:

What is the purpose of a fuse in an electrical circuit?

A) To store electrical energy B) To increase the current C) To prevent circuit overload D) To decrease resistance

Answer: C) To prevent circuit overload

Explanation: A fuse is a safety device designed to protect an electrical circuit from damage caused by an excess current, typically resulting from an overload or short circuit. Its essential component is a metal wire or strip that melts when too much current flows through it, thereby interrupting the current.

26. Question:

What is the main function of a transistor in an electrical circuit?

A) To convert AC to DC B) To convert DC to AC C) To amplify or switch electronic signals D) To reduce voltage

Answer: C) To amplify or switch electronic signals

Explanation: The main function of a transistor in an electrical circuit is to amplify or switch electronic signals.

27. Question:

Which law states that the sum of currents entering a junction must equal the sum of currents leaving the junction?

A) Ohm's Law B) Kirchhoff's Current Law C) Faraday's Law D) Gauss's Law

Answer: B) Kirchhoff's Current Law

Explanation: Kirchhoff's Current Law states that the sum of currents entering a junction in an electrical circuit must equal the sum of currents leaving the junction.

28. Question:

What is the unit of measure for inductance?

A) Ohm B) Henry C) Farad D) Ampere

Answer: B) Henry

Explanation: The unit of measure for inductance is the Henry.

29. Question:

What happens to the brightness of a light bulb if the voltage across it is increased?

A) The brightness increases B) The brightness decreases C) The brightness stays the same D) The bulb burns out

Answer: A) The brightness increases

Explanation: The brightness of a light bulb increases if the voltage across it is increased, assuming the bulb doesn't reach its maximum capacity and burn out.

30. Question:

In a parallel circuit with two resistors, if the resistance of one resistor is doubled, what happens to the total resistance?

A) It doubles B) It halves C) It decreases, but doesn't halve D) It increases, but doesn't double

Answer: C) It decreases, but doesn't halve

Explanation: In a parallel circuit, if the resistance of one resistor is doubled, the total resistance of the circuit decreases, but it doesn't halve. In a parallel circuit, the total resistance is less than the resistance of the smallest resistor.

31. Question:

What does the term "semi-conductor" refer to in electronics?

A) A device that only conducts electricity in one direction B) A device that converts AC to DC C) A material that has resistance levels between that of a conductor and an insulator D) A device that boosts the signal strength of an electronic device

Answer: C) A material that has resistance levels between that of a conductor and an insulator

Explanation: In electronics, a semiconductor refers to a material that has resistance levels between that of a conductor and an insulator. Semiconductors are the foundation of modern electronics, including transistors, solar cells, LEDs, and integrated circuits.

32. Question:

What is the total resistance of two 10 ohm resistors connected in parallel?

A) 5 ohms B) 10 ohms C) 20 ohms D) 40 ohms

Answer: A) 5 ohms

Explanation: When resistors are connected in parallel, their total equivalent resistance (Req) can be calculated using the formula 1/Req = 1/R1 + 1/R2. For two 10 ohm resistors, this gives 1/Req = 1/10 + 1/10 = 2/10. Taking the reciprocal gives Req = 10/2 = 5 ohms.

33. Question:

What is the purpose of a diode in an electronic circuit?

A) To store electrical charge B) To allow current to flow in one direction only C) To reduce resistance D) To increase voltage

Answer: B) To allow current to flow in one direction only

Explanation: A diode is a component in an electronic circuit that primarily allows current to flow in one direction only. This unidirectional behavior is called rectification.

34. Question:

In a DC circuit, what is the relationship between power (P), voltage (V), and current (I)?

A) P = VI B) P = V/I C) P = I/V D) P = V + I

Answer: A) P = VI

Explanation: In a DC circuit, the relationship between power (P), voltage (V), and current (I) is P = VI, which is known as Joule's law.

35. Question:

What is the primary function of a transformer in an electronic circuit?

A) To convert AC to DC B) To allow current to flow in one direction only C) To change the voltage level D) To limit current flow

Answer: C) To change the voltage level

Explanation: The primary function of a transformer in an electronic circuit is to change the voltage level. This is typically done by using magnetic induction between coils to convert higher voltage electricity to lower voltage electricity, and vice versa.

36. Question:

In a series circuit with three resistors, if the current through the circuit is constant, which of the following is true?

A) The voltage drop across each resistor is the same B) The voltage drop across each resistor is different C) The total resistance is the sum of the individual resistances D) Both B and C

Answer: D) Both B and C

Explanation: In a series circuit with a constant current, the voltage drop across each resistor is different and depends on the resistance of each component according to Ohm's Law (V = IR). The total resistance in a series circuit is indeed the sum of the individual resistances.

37. Question:

What is the unit of frequency?

A) Ampere B) Volt C) Ohm D) Hertz

Answer: D) Hertz

Explanation: The unit of frequency is Hertz (Hz).

38. Question:

What type of circuit is used to control the speed of a motor?

A) Series circuit B) Parallel circuit C) Resistor-capacitor (RC) circuit D) Resistor-inductor (RL) circuit

Answer: D) Resistor-inductor (RL) circuit

Explanation: A Resistor-Inductor (RL) circuit is often used to control the speed of a motor. In an RL circuit, the resistor (R) limits the amount of current that can flow through the circuit, and the inductor (L) can store energy, which can then be released back into the circuit. By changing the resistance, you can control how much current flows through the motor, thus controlling the speed of the motor.

39. Question:

What is the electrical charge of a neutron?

A) Positive B) Negative C) Neutral D) It depends on the context

Answer: C) Neutral

Explanation: A neutron, one of the three main particles in an atom along with protons and electrons, carries no electrical charge and is therefore neutral.

40. Question:

Which component in an electronic circuit is used to limit the flow of current?

A) Diode B) Resistor C) Inductor D) Capacitor

Answer: B) Resistor

Explanation: In an electronic circuit, a resistor is used to limit the flow of current. It achieves this by providing a certain amount of resistance to the flow of current, in accordance with Ohm's Law.

41. Question:

What does the capacitor do in an electronic circuit?

A) It allows current to flow in one direction only B) It converts AC to DC C) It stores electrical energy D) It resists the flow of current

Answer: C) It stores electrical energy

Explanation: In an electronic circuit, a capacitor is used to store electrical energy in an electric field. This stored energy can be released into the circuit when needed.

42. Question:

Which electrical device converts mechanical energy into electrical energy?

A) Motor B) Generator C) Resistor D) Capacitor

Answer: B) Generator

Explanation: A generator is an electrical device that converts mechanical energy into electrical energy. This is typically achieved through electromagnetic induction.

43. Question:

Which electronic component can amplify signals?

A) Diode B) Resistor C) Transistor D) Inductor

Answer: C) Transistor

Explanation: A transistor, which can function as an amplifier, is an electronic component that can amplify signals. It can also be used as a switch.

44. Question:

What is Ohm's Law?

A) The current in a circuit is directly proportional to the voltage and inversely proportional to the resistance B) The voltage in a circuit is directly proportional to the current and inversely proportional to the resistance C) The resistance in a circuit is directly proportional to the voltage and inversely proportional to the current D)

The voltage in a circuit is equal to the product of the current and resistance

Answer: D) The voltage in a circuit is equal to the product of the current and resistance

Explanation: Ohm's Law states that the voltage (V) across a resistor is equal to the product of the current (I) flowing through it and its resistance (R). This is often expressed as V = IR.

45. Question:

What is the color code for a resistor with a value of 100 ohms?

A) Red, Black, Brown, Gold B) Brown, Black, Black, Gold C) Brown, Black, Brown, Gold D) Red, Black, Red, Gold

Answer: C) Brown, Black, Brown, Gold

Explanation: In the standard color-coding scheme for resistors, a 100-ohm resistor would be Brown (1), Black (0), Brown (multiplier of 10^1), and Gold (±5% tolerance).

46. Question:

In a parallel circuit, what happens to the total resistance if you add another resistor?

A) It increases B) It decreases C) It remains the same D) It doubles

Answer: B) It decreases

Explanation: In a parallel circuit, adding another resistor actually decreases the total resistance. This is because the total resistance in a parallel circuit is given by the reciprocal of the sum of the reciprocals of the individual resistances.

47. Question:

What is the function of a fuse in an electronic circuit?

A) To store charge B) To allow current to flow in one direction only C) To protect the circuit from excessive current D) To increase the current flow

Answer: C) To protect the circuit from excessive current

Explanation: The primary function of a fuse in an electronic circuit is to protect the circuit from excessive current. The fuse contains a piece of wire that melts and breaks the circuit if the current exceeds a certain level.

48. Question:

What is the symbol for a ground in an electronic circuit diagram?

A) A straight line B) A triangle C) Three horizontal lines getting smaller as they go down D) A circle

Answer: C) Three horizontal lines getting smaller as they go down

Explanation: In an electronic circuit diagram, the symbol for a ground (or earth) is three horizontal lines that get smaller as they go down.

49. Question:

What type of device is a photodiode?

A) A device that generates a voltage when exposed to light B) A device that emits light when a voltage is applied C) A device that stores energy when exposed to light D) A device that resists current when exposed to light

Answer: A) A device that generates a voltage when exposed to light

Explanation: A photodiode is a type of device that generates a voltage when it is exposed to light. This is due to the photoelectric effect.

50. Question:

What is the unit of electrical power?

A) Joule B) Ohm C) Watt D) Ampere

Answer: C) Watt

Explanation: The unit of electrical power is the Watt (W), named after the Scottish engineer James Watt. One watt is equivalent to one joule per second.

Test Strategies

Electronics Information is a key section of the ASVAB that measures your understanding of electrical equipment and devices, and basic electronic principles. Here are some strategies that you can use to improve your performance in this section.

1. Understand the Basics: Before you even start practicing, ensure you have a solid understanding of the basics of electronics. This includes knowing common terms, such as voltage, current, and resistance, as well as understanding basic principles, such as Ohm's Law and how circuits work.

2. Learn the Components: Electronic circuits are made up of various components, such as resistors, capacitors, inductors, and diodes. Each of these components has a specific symbol that is used to represent it in circuit diagrams. Being able to recognize these symbols and knowing the function of each component will be very helpful.

3. Study Color Codes: Resistors are color-coded to indicate their resistance value. Learning this color code can be helpful for questions that ask about a resistor's value. Remember the mnemonic "BBROYGBVGW" to recall the color code sequence: Black, Brown, Red, Orange, Yellow, Green, Blue, Violet, Gray, White.

4. Practice Circuit Analysis: Many questions will present you with a circuit diagram and ask you to determine certain values, such as the total resistance, current, or voltage. To do these types of problems, you need to know how to analyze a circuit. This includes understanding series and parallel circuits, knowing how to calculate total resistance, and knowing how to apply Ohm's Law and Kirchhoff's laws.

5. Understand the Function of Devices: You'll likely encounter questions about the function of certain electronic devices, such as transistors, diodes, and transformers. Make sure you understand what each device does and how it works within a circuit.

6. Practice, Practice, Practice: Lastly, and perhaps most importantly, practice! The more practice questions you do, the more familiar you'll become with the types of questions you'll see on the test, and the better you'll get at answering them. Practice tests will also help you identify areas where you need more study.

Remember, the ASVAB is a timed test, so you should also practice answering questions quickly and accurately. Try to develop a strategy for dealing with difficult questions - for example, if you can't figure out the answer, eliminate as many wrong choices as you can and then take your best guess.

By following these strategies, you'll be well-prepared for the Electronics Information section of the ASVAB. Good luck with your study!

Chapter 8

Auto and Shop Information

Overview and Study Guide

The Auto and Shop Information subtest is part of the Armed Services Vocational Aptitude Battery (ASVAB) that measures your knowledge and understanding of vehicle maintenance, repairs, and shop principles. Here's what you need to know:

Auto Information

This section tests your knowledge of automobiles and automobile maintenance. It covers a variety of topics, including:

1. **Engine Systems:** Understanding the different components of an engine and their functions is crucial. This includes the fuel system, cooling system, lubrication system, ignition system, and exhaust system. You should know basic engine terminology like pistons, crankshaft, camshaft, and cylinders.

2. **Transmission:** You should understand how both automatic and manual transmissions work. This

includes knowing the role of the clutch, torque converter, gears, and shift linkage.

3. **Brakes:** Understanding the basic components of a braking system, such as the brake pedal, master cylinder, brake lines, drums, pads, and shoes, is essential. You should also know about both disc brakes and drum brakes.

4. **Electrical Systems:** You will need to know about a car's electrical system, including the battery, alternator, starter motor, and wiring. Also, understanding how headlights, taillights, and turn signals function can be beneficial.

5. **Wheels and Tires:** Understanding the types of tires, their construction, and various tire maintenance procedures, such as rotation and alignment, can be expected.

Shop Information

This section tests your understanding of basic shop principles and practices. Topics covered include:

1. **Hand Tools:** You should know the names, uses, and safety measures associated with various hand

tools, such as hammers, screwdrivers, pliers, wrenches, and saws.

2. **Power Tools:** Knowing about power tools like drills, grinders, and circular saws is also important. This includes understanding their uses and safety precautions.

3. **Shop Safety:** You'll need to know basic safety rules for working in a shop, such as using safety glasses, handling chemicals, and using tools properly.

4. **Shop Math:** Basic arithmetic and its application to shop scenarios are part of this test. This can include measuring lengths, calculating areas and volumes, and understanding angles.

5. **Shop Terminology and Procedures:** Understand common shop terms and procedures. This can include understanding plans and diagrams, knowing the order of operations for common tasks, and knowing basic troubleshooting methods.

To perform well on the Auto and Shop Information subtest, you'll need to study and understand these topics. Practical experience can be incredibly beneficial, so if you have the opportunity to work on a car or in a shop, take advantage of it. Reading books, watching videos, and taking practice tests can also help reinforce your knowledge.

Practice Test with Answers

1. Question:

What is the function of a car's alternator?

A) To ignite the fuel-air mixture in the engine B) To change gears while driving C) To supply electricity to the car's systems and recharge the battery D) To filter impurities out of the oil

Answer: C) To supply electricity to the car's systems and recharge the battery

Explanation: The alternator in a car is used to generate electricity for the car's electrical systems and recharge the battery while the engine is running.

2. Question:

What tool would you use to tighten or loosen bolts?

A) Pliers B) Wrench C) Hammer D) Screwdriver

Answer: B) Wrench

Explanation: A wrench is a tool used to provide grip and mechanical advantage in applying torque to turn objects, usually rotary fasteners, such as nuts and bolts.

3. Question:

What is the function of the radiator in a car?

A) Lubrication B) Ignition C) Cooling D) Fuel Supply

Answer: C) Cooling

Explanation: The radiator is a part of the cooling system in a car. It helps keep the engine from overheating by dissipating the heat produced by the engine.

4. Question:

What type of braking system uses a hydraulic fluid to transmit pressure from the controlling mechanism to the braking mechanism?

A) Friction braking system B) Drum braking system C) Disc braking system D) Hydraulic braking system

Answer: D) Hydraulic braking system

Explanation: A hydraulic braking system uses hydraulic fluid to transmit pressure from the control mechanisms to the braking mechanism.

5. Question:

What is the purpose of the transmission in a car?

A) To convert the engine's power into movement B) To start the engine C) To cool the engine D) To control the electrical systems

Answer: A) To convert the engine's power into movement

Explanation: The purpose of the transmission is to convert the power generated by the engine into movement by transferring it to the wheels.

6. Question:

What should you do if you spill a chemical in the shop?

A) Leave it for someone else to clean up B) Clean it up immediately following proper safety procedures C) Ignore it if it's a small spill D) Pour water on it to dilute it

Answer: B) Clean it up immediately following proper safety procedures

Explanation: Spills in the shop, especially chemical spills, should be cleaned up immediately following safety procedures to prevent accidents and injuries.

7. Question:

What is the purpose of a timing belt or chain in an engine?

A) To control the opening and closing of the engine's valves B) To pump fuel into the engine C) To provide electricity to the engine D) To cool the engine

Answer: A) To control the opening and closing of the engine's valves

Explanation: The timing belt or chain in an engine is responsible for controlling the timing of the engine's valves, ensuring they open and close at the correct times during each cylinder's intake and exhaust strokes.

8. Question:

Which of the following is NOT a type of screwdriver?

A) Flathead B) Phillips C) Pliers D) Torx

Answer: C) Pliers

Explanation: Pliers are a type of tool used for gripping, bending, and cutting, not a type of screwdriver. Flathead, Phillips, and Torx are all types of screwdrivers.

9. Question:

Which safety equipment should be used when grinding metal?

A) Safety goggles B) Ear plugs C) Dust mask D) All of the above

Answer: D) All of the above

Explanation: When grinding metal, small particles can become airborne and cause injury to the eyes, ears, and lungs. Therefore, it's important to wear safety goggles, ear plugs, and a dust mask.

10. Question:

What is the correct order of operation for starting a car with a manual transmission?

A) Press clutch, turn key, release clutch B) Turn key, press clutch, release clutch C) Press clutch, release clutch, turn key D) Release clutch, press clutch, turn key

Answer: A) Press clutch, turn key, release clutch

Explanation: To start a car with a manual transmission, you first press the clutch to disengage the transmission, then you turn the key to start the engine. Once the engine is running, you can slowly release the clutch to engage the transmission.

11. Question:

Which part of a car uses a mixture of water and antifreeze to cool the engine?

A) Alternator B) Transmission C) Radiator D) Distributor

Answer: C) Radiator

Explanation: The radiator uses a mixture of water and antifreeze to absorb heat from the engine and then cool it down.

12. Question:

Which of these tools is most appropriate for holding a small nail while hammering?

A) Wrench B) Pliers C) Screwdriver D) Socket

Answer: B) Pliers

Explanation: Pliers can hold a small nail securely while you hammer, reducing the risk of injury to your fingers.

13. Question:

What is the purpose of the muffler in a car's exhaust system?

A) Increase fuel efficiency B) Reduce the noise produced by the exhaust C) Filter impurities from the exhaust D) Cool down the exhaust gases

Answer: B) Reduce the noise produced by the exhaust

Explanation: The muffler's primary function in a car's exhaust system is to reduce the noise produced by the exhaust gases.

14. Question:

In a vehicle, what does the term "4WD" stand for?

A) 4 Wheel Drive B) 4 Wheel Drift C) 4 Wheel Diameter D) 4 Wheel Distance

Answer: A) 4 Wheel Drive

Explanation: "4WD" stands for "Four-Wheel Drive," a type of drivetrain that allows all four wheels of a vehicle to receive torque from the engine simultaneously.

15. Question:

In the context of shop safety, what is the purpose of a Material Safety Data Sheet (MSDS)?

A) To provide a catalog of all shop tools B) To provide information about materials, including how to use them safely C) To provide a record of all materials purchased D) To provide an inventory of all shop materials

Answer: B) To provide information about materials, including how to use them safely

Explanation: A Material Safety Data Sheet (MSDS) provides detailed information about a specific material or chemical product, including how to use, store, and dispose of it safely.

16. Question:

What is the main purpose of engine oil in a car?

A) To cool the engine B) To lubricate the engine's moving parts C) To clean the engine D) All of the above

Answer: D) All of the above

Explanation: Engine oil has multiple functions in a car: it lubricates the moving parts of the engine to reduce friction and wear, it helps to cool the engine by carrying away heat, and it also cleans the engine by carrying away dirt, soot, and other contaminants.

17. Question:

What is a serpentine belt in a car engine used for?

A) To transmit power to the engine accessories B) To time the opening and closing of the engine valves C) To connect the wheels to the transmission D) To deliver fuel to the engine

Answer: A) To transmit power to the engine accessories

Explanation: A serpentine belt is a single, continuous belt used to drive multiple peripheral devices in an automotive engine, such as an alternator, power steering pump, water pump, air conditioning compressor, and others.

18. Question:

What is the purpose of the carburetor in a car engine?

A) To supply fuel to the engine B) To cool the engine C) To filter the engine oil D) To ignite the fuel-air mixture

Answer: A) To supply fuel to the engine

Explanation: The carburetor's main function in a car engine is to mix air and fuel in the correct ratio for combustion.

19. Question:

What does a spark plug do in a car engine?

A) It ignites the fuel-air mixture B) It cools the engine C) It filters the engine oil D) It delivers electricity to the battery

Answer: A) It ignites the fuel-air mixture

Explanation: The spark plug in a car engine delivers an electric current from the ignition system to the combustion chamber to ignite the fuel-air mixture and start the power stroke of the engine cycle.

20. Question:

When painting a surface, what is the purpose of primer?

A) To give the paint a smooth surface to adhere to B) To protect the surface from the paint C) To give the paint a shiny finish D) To thin the paint

Answer: A) To give the paint a smooth surface to adhere to

Explanation: The primary purpose of primer is to prepare (prime) the surface for painting. It provides a smooth surface for the paint to adhere to and can also seal the surface and prevent stains or darker colors from showing through the paint.

21. Question:

Which tool would you use to measure the diameter of a pipe?

A) A tape measure B) A ruler C) A caliper D) A protractor

Answer: C) A caliper

Explanation: A caliper is a tool that can measure the external or internal diameter of an object, such as a pipe. It is more accurate for this purpose than a ruler or a tape measure.

22. Question:

What is the purpose of a fuse in an electrical system?

A) To increase the voltage B) To prevent electrical overload C) To store electrical energy D) To convert AC to DC

Answer: B) To prevent electrical overload

Explanation: A fuse is a protective device in an electrical circuit that melts and breaks the circuit if the current exceeds a specified value, preventing damage from electrical overload.

23. Question:

What is a catalytic converter used for in a car?

A) Increasing fuel efficiency B) Reducing harmful emissions C) Amplifying engine sound D) Cooling the engine

Answer: B) Reducing harmful emissions

Explanation: A catalytic converter is a device in the exhaust system of a car that uses catalysts to convert harmful gases into less harmful substances before they are emitted from the exhaust.

24. Question:

Which type of oil would be most suitable for a high-temperature engine?

A) Low viscosity oil B) High viscosity oil C) Any type of oil D) Oil-free lubricant

Answer: B) High viscosity oil

Explanation: High viscosity oil is thicker and better able to maintain its lubricating properties at high temperatures, making it suitable for a high-temperature engine.

25. Question:

What type of screwdriver would you use to tighten a Phillips head screw?

A) Flathead screwdriver B) Phillips screwdriver C) Hex screwdriver D) Torx screwdriver

Answer: B) Phillips screwdriver

Explanation: A Phillips screwdriver has a cross-shaped tip that fits into the cross-shaped recess of a Phillips head screw, allowing you to tighten or loosen the screw.

26. Question:

What is a multimeter used for?

A) Measuring multiple dimensions of an object B) Measuring multiple properties of electrical circuits C)

Measuring multiple types of materials D) Measuring multiple weights at once

Answer: B) Measuring multiple properties of electrical circuits

Explanation: A multimeter is a tool that can measure multiple properties of electrical circuits, including voltage, current, and resistance.

27. Question:

Which type of wrench would you use to tighten a hexagonal bolt?

A) Crescent wrench B) Box-end wrench C) Pipe wrench D) Torque wrench

Answer: B) Box-end wrench

Explanation: A box-end wrench has a closed loop (or "box") at one or both ends that fits over a nut or bolt. This design provides a good grip on the fastener, making it an ideal choice for hexagonal bolts.

28. Question:

Which tool would you use to create a hole in a piece of wood?

A) Saw B) Drill C) Hammer D) Screwdriver

Answer: B) Drill

Explanation: A drill is a tool that uses a rotating drill bit to create holes in various materials, including wood.

29. Question:

What is the function of the alternator in a car?

A) To start the engine B) To charge the battery and power the electrical system while the engine is running C) To control the air conditioning system D) To control the transmission

Answer: B) To charge the battery and power the electrical system while the engine is running

Explanation: The alternator generates electrical power to run the car's electrical systems and recharge the battery while the engine is running.

30. Question:

What is the purpose of sandpaper?

A) To polish a surface B) To remove material from a surface C) To apply paint to a surface D) To measure the dimensions of a surface

Answer: B) To remove material from a surface

Explanation: Sandpaper is used to remove small amounts of material from surfaces, usually in preparation for painting, varnishing, or otherwise finishing the surface. It can also be used to roughen a smooth surface, making it easier for things like glue or paint to adhere.

31. Question:

What type of paint would you use on a surface that is exposed to high temperatures, such as a grill or stove?

A) Latex paint B) Oil-based paint C) Heat-resistant paint D) Enamel paint

Answer: C) Heat-resistant paint

Explanation: Heat-resistant paint is designed to withstand high temperatures without peeling, cracking, or fading, making it suitable for surfaces that are exposed to high temperatures, like grills and stoves.

32. Question:

What does a jack do in a car?

A) It changes the tires B) It lifts the car C) It powers the car D) It cools the engine

Answer: B) It lifts the car

Explanation: A car jack is a device used to raise a vehicle off the ground so that maintenance or repairs, such as changing a tire, can be performed.

33. Question:

What is the purpose of an oil filter in a car engine?

A) To remove impurities from the oil B) To cool the oil C) To increase the oil pressure D) To monitor the oil level

Answer: A) To remove impurities from the oil

Explanation: An oil filter's main job is to clean out any small particles of dirt or metal that may have made it into the oil, preventing them from damaging the engine.

34. Question:

Which tool would you use to cut a metal pipe?

A) A hacksaw B) A hammer C) A wrench D) A screwdriver

Answer: A) A hacksaw

Explanation: A hacksaw is a type of saw that's used for cutting metal.

35. Question:

What is a timing belt in a car engine?

A) A belt that controls the timing of the engine's valves B) A belt that drives the alternator C) A belt that controls the air conditioning system D) A belt that connects the engine to the transmission

Answer: A) A belt that controls the timing of the engine's valves

Explanation: The timing belt is a component of an internal combustion engine that synchronizes the rotation of the crankshaft and the camshaft(s) so that the engine's valves open and close at the correct times during each cylinder's intake and exhaust strokes.

36. Question:

What type of tool is a pliers?

A) A cutting tool B) A measuring tool C) A gripping tool D) A shaping tool

Answer: C) A gripping tool

Explanation: Pliers are primarily used for gripping and manipulating objects. They can also be used for bending, cutting, and shaping various materials.

37. Question:

What is the purpose of a radiator in a car?

A) To cool the engine B) To filter the engine oil C) To provide heat for the passenger compartment D) To power the air conditioning system

Answer: A) To cool the engine

Explanation: The radiator's primary role is to keep the engine cool by transferring heat from the coolant that flows through it to the air blown through it by the fan.

38. Question:

What is a voltmeter used for?

A) To measure resistance in an electrical circuit B) To measure current in an electrical circuit C) To measure voltage in an electrical circuit D) To measure the power output of an electrical circuit

Answer: C) To measure voltage in an electrical circuit

Explanation: A voltmeter is an instrument used for measuring the electrical potential difference, also known as voltage, between two points in an electrical or electronic circuit.

39. Question:

What is the purpose of the brake fluid in a car?

A) To cool the brake pads B) To lubricate the brake pads C) To transmit force from the brake pedal to the brake pads D) To clean the brake pads

Answer: C) To transmit force from the brake pedal to the brake pads

Explanation: Brake fluid is a type of hydraulic fluid that is used to transmit the force of the driver's foot on the brake pedal into pressure which then stops the car.

40. Question:

Which tool would be best to use to turn a bolt with a hexagonal head?

A) Screwdriver B) Pliers C) Wrench D) Hammer

Answer: C) Wrench

Explanation: A wrench (specifically a hex or socket wrench) is the appropriate tool for turning a hexagonal bolt head. It is designed to fit around the hexagonal shape and provide the necessary leverage for turning.

41. Question:

Which type of automotive fluid is typically red?

A) Brake fluid B) Power steering fluid C) Transmission fluid D) Engine coolant

Answer: C) Transmission fluid

Explanation: Transmission fluid is typically red. It serves as a lubricant for the transmission's moving parts and also helps to maintain the correct pressure needed for the transmission to function properly.

42. Question:

Which part of the car is responsible for converting exhaust gases into less harmful substances?

A) Muffler B) Radiator C) Catalytic converter D) Carburetor

Answer: C) Catalytic converter

Explanation: The catalytic converter is part of a vehicle's exhaust system and is responsible for converting harmful gases into less harmful substances before they are emitted from the exhaust pipe.

43. Question:

What is the purpose of a fuse in an electrical circuit?

A) To increase the current B) To store electrical energy C) To protect the circuit from an overload D) To convert AC current to DC current

Answer: C) To protect the circuit from an overload

Explanation: A fuse is a safety device that protects an electrical circuit from excessive current, which can cause damage or potentially start a fire. If the current running through the circuit exceeds the rated level, the fuse 'blows,' or melts, breaking the circuit and stopping the flow of electricity.

44. Question:

What is the function of a spark plug in a car engine?

A) To ignite the air-fuel mixture B) To lubricate the pistons C) To cool the engine D) To filter the engine oil

Answer: A) To ignite the air-fuel mixture

Explanation: The spark plug's main function in a car engine is to ignite the air-fuel mixture in the combustion chamber, creating the combustion that powers the engine.

45. Question:

Which tool is used to hold and turn nuts and bolts?

A) Screwdriver B) Pliers C) Wrench D) Hammer

Answer: C) Wrench

Explanation: A wrench is a tool used to provide grip and mechanical advantage in applying torque to turn objects—usually rotary fasteners, such as nuts and bolts—or to keep them from turning.

46. Question:

In welding, what does an acetylene torch do?

A) It cools down metal B) It cuts metal C) It polishes metal D) It measures metal thickness

Answer: B) It cuts metal

Explanation: An acetylene torch can be used for cutting metal, as well as for welding (joining metals together). The torch produces a flame hot enough to melt metal, allowing it to be cut or shaped as needed.

47. Question:

What is a car's differential used for?

A) It distributes engine power to the wheels B) It cools the engine C) It charges the battery D) It filters the engine oil

Answer: A) It distributes engine power to the wheels

Explanation: A differential is a device that splits the engine torque in two directions, allowing each output to spin at a different speed. It's crucial in turns, where the inside wheel travels a shorter distance than the outside wheel.

48. Question:

What type of tool is a miter saw?

A) A cutting tool B) A measuring tool C) A gripping tool D) A shaping tool

Answer: A) A cutting tool

Explanation: A miter saw is a tool used for making accurate crosscuts and miters in a workpiece by positioning a mounted blade onto a board in a quick downward motion.

49. Question:

What does the alternator do in a car?

A) It generates electrical power B) It cools the engine C) It pumps brake fluid D) It filters the engine oil

Answer: A) It generates electrical power

Explanation: The alternator's role in a car is to generate electrical power for various systems and to recharge the battery while the car's engine is running.

50. Question:

What is the name of the tool used to measure tire pressure?

A) Pressure gauge B) Torque wrench C) Micrometer D) Tire iron

Answer: A) Pressure gauge

Explanation: A pressure gauge, specifically a tire pressure gauge, is used to measure the air pressure inside a tire. Regularly checking and maintaining proper tire pressure is important for safety, optimal vehicle performance, and fuel efficiency.

Test Strategies

The Auto and Shop Information section of the ASVAB test is designed to measure your knowledge and familiarity with automobile technology and basic shop practices. It is an essential part of the examination for individuals looking to join technical departments in the Navy or other branches of the military.

Developing effective test strategies is crucial to optimize your study and test-taking efforts, and to ultimately achieve a high score in this section. Below are some recommended strategies that can help.

1. Understand the Basics:

While it's impossible to predict the exact questions that will appear on the test, the Auto and Shop Information section typically covers the same fundamental concepts related to auto mechanics, shop terminology, and tool use. Spend time studying and understanding these concepts, and you should be well-prepared for the variety of questions that can be asked.

2. Familiarize Yourself with Tools and Their Uses:

A significant part of this test section includes questions about different tools and their uses. Make sure you are familiar with a wide range of hand tools, power tools, and measuring devices. Knowing the correct application of these tools can be a significant advantage.

3. Learn Basic Automotive Systems:

A basic understanding of the different systems in a vehicle—such as the braking system, transmission system, electrical system, and cooling system—will help you answer questions related to auto information. Try to learn how these systems work and what each part's function is.

4. Understand Shop Terminology:

In addition to automotive knowledge, the test includes questions about basic shop practices and terminologies. Knowing common practices and procedures in a workshop, as well as safety protocols, can help improve your score.

5. Practice, Practice, Practice:

Just like any other test, practice is key to success. Use practice tests to familiarize yourself with the question format and to identify areas where you may need more study.

6. Use Process of Elimination:

During the test, if you encounter a difficult question, use the process of elimination to rule out incorrect answers. This strategy increases your chances of choosing the correct answer.

7. Time Management:

The Auto and Shop Information section consists of 25 questions that you need to answer in 11 minutes. It's essential to monitor your time to ensure you answer all questions. Practice speed reading and quick comprehension to help manage your time better during the test.

8. Stay Calm:

Test anxiety can negatively affect your performance. Make sure to relax and stay calm during your test. Take deep breaths, read each question carefully, and believe in your preparation.

Remember, the ASVAB test doesn't penalize you for wrong answers, so make sure to answer all questions. With a solid understanding of auto and shop information, good test strategies, and sufficient practice, you'll be well-equipped to score high in this section of the ASVAB.

Chapter 9
Mechanical Comprehension

Overview and Study Guide

The Mechanical Comprehension section of the Armed Services Vocational Aptitude Battery (ASVAB) test assesses your understanding of basic mechanical principles and mechanisms. It's often considered one of the more challenging parts of the ASVAB, but with a thorough understanding of key concepts and adequate preparation, you can approach this section with confidence.

Overview

Mechanical Comprehension involves topics related to the principles of mechanical devices, structural support, properties of materials, and fluid dynamics. You'll be asked to identify various mechanical tools and devices, understand their functions, and analyze the forces acting on them. You'll also need to understand the relationship between force, mass, and acceleration, along with the laws of motion.

Study Guide

As you prepare for the Mechanical Comprehension section of the ASVAB, consider the following areas of focus:

1. Principles of Mechanics:

Study the basic principles of mechanics, including Newton's Laws of Motion. Understand the concepts of force, pressure, energy, work, power, and torque. Familiarize yourself with simple machines, like levers, pulleys, gears, and inclined planes, and understand how they work.

2. Understanding of Mechanical Tools:

Be able to identify common mechanical tools and know their uses. This could include a variety of hand and power tools.

3. Fluid Dynamics:

This involves understanding the principles of liquid and gas flow, and concepts like buoyancy, pressure, and the basics of hydraulic systems.

4. Basic Physical Sciences:

A basic understanding of the physical sciences, particularly physics, is helpful. This includes knowledge of principles like gravity, friction, velocity, acceleration, and density.

5. Spatial Awareness:

Some questions might involve visualizing the movement of mechanical parts. Being able to visualize spatial relationships and movements can be very helpful.

6. Material Properties:

Understanding different types of materials, their properties, and their uses in mechanical applications is often required. This could include metals, plastics, and other common materials.

7. Electrical Basics:

While it's not the focus of this section, a basic understanding of electrical principles can be helpful. This might include simple electrical circuits, electrical units of measurement, and understanding voltage, current, and resistance.

As part of your study regimen, practice tests can be incredibly valuable. They help familiarize you with the test format and question types, while also allowing you to assess your strengths and weaknesses. Be sure to review both correct and incorrect answers to understand the principles behind each question.

Remember, this test assesses your understanding of mechanical principles, not your memorization of facts. Understanding why things work the way they do will be far more beneficial than merely trying to remember specific details. By focusing on comprehension, you'll be better equipped to tackle the variety of questions that may appear on the ASVAB Mechanical Comprehension test.

Practice Test with Answers

1. Question:

What is Newton's First Law of Motion also known as?

A) Law of Acceleration B) Law of Inertia C) Law of Gravitation D) Law of Momentum

Answer: B) Law of Inertia

Explanation: Newton's First Law of Motion, also known as the Law of Inertia, states that an object at rest will stay at rest, and an object in motion will stay in motion with the same speed and in the same direction unless acted upon by an unbalanced force.

2. Question:

What type of simple machine is a see-saw?

A) Wheel and axle B) Lever C) Pulley D) Inclined plane

Answer: B) Lever

Explanation: A see-saw is an example of a lever, a simple machine that involves a bar that pivots at a fixed point called a fulcrum.

3. Question:

In hydraulic systems, the fluid used is nearly incompressible. True or false?

A) True B) False

Answer: A) True

Explanation: In hydraulic systems, fluids like oil are used because they are nearly incompressible, allowing them to transmit pressure throughout the system effectively.

4. Question:

What determines the amount of friction between two surfaces?

A) The types of materials and the amount of surface in contact B) The temperature of the materials C) The color of the materials D) The age of the materials

Answer: A) The types of materials and the amount of surface in contact

Explanation: Friction depends on the types of materials in contact and the amount of surface area in contact. Other factors can also influence friction, such as the smoothness of the surfaces and the forces pressing them together.

5. Question:

What is the unit of measurement for electrical resistance?

A) Watt B) Volt C) Ampere D) Ohm

Answer: D) Ohm

Explanation: The unit of measurement for electrical resistance is the ohm, symbolized by Ω.

6. Question:

Which of the following is an example of a wheel and axle?

A) Screwdriver B) Door knob C) Stairs D) Pulley

Answer: B) Door knob

Explanation: A door knob is an example of a wheel and axle. When you turn the knob (the wheel), it turns the rod or spindle (the axle), which moves the latch.

7. Question:

What is the term for the amount of matter in an object?

A) Weight B) Volume C) Mass D) Density

Answer: C) Mass

Explanation: The mass of an object refers to the amount of matter it contains.

8. Question:

What do we call a force that resists the relative motion of two contacting surfaces?

A) Inertia B) Momentum C) Gravity D) Friction

Answer: D) Friction

Explanation: Friction is the force that resists the relative motion of two contacting surfaces.

9. Question:

What is the mechanical advantage of a lever when the effort arm is three times longer than the resistance arm?

A) 1 B) 2 C) 3 D) 4

Answer: C) 3

Explanation: The mechanical advantage of a lever is the ratio of the length of the effort arm to the length of the resistance arm. If the effort arm is three times longer than the resistance arm, the mechanical advantage is 3.

10. Question:

A buoyant force acts in the opposite direction to gravity. True or false?

A) True B) False

Answer: A) True

Explanation: Buoyant force acts in the opposite direction to gravity. It's the force exerted on an object that is wholly or partly immersed in a fluid, pushing it up.

11. Question:

Which of the following materials is a good conductor of electricity?

A) Rubber B) Plastic C) Wood D) Copper

Answer: D) Copper

Explanation: Copper is an excellent conductor of electricity, and it is commonly used in electrical wiring.

12. Question:

How does an increase in temperature generally affect the viscosity of a liquid?

A) Increases viscosity B) Decreases viscosity C) No effect on viscosity D) Depends on the type of liquid

Answer: B) Decreases viscosity

Explanation: In general, as the temperature of a liquid increases, its viscosity decreases. That means the liquid flows more easily at higher temperatures.

13. Question:

What force is responsible for an object falling to the ground when dropped?

A) Friction B) Inertia C) Gravity D) Buoyancy

Answer: C) Gravity

Explanation: Gravity is the force that pulls objects toward the center of the earth. When you drop an object, it falls to the ground because of gravity.

14. Question:

Which simple machine would be most useful for raising a heavy object straight off the ground?

A) Lever B) Screw C) Inclined plane D) Pulley

Answer: D) Pulley

Explanation: A pulley can change the direction of the applied force and makes it easier to lift heavy objects straight off the ground.

15. Question:

If an object is at rest and stays at rest, what can be said about the forces acting on it?

A) There are no forces acting on it B) There is only one force acting on it C) The forces acting on it are unbalanced D) The forces acting on it are balanced

Answer: D) The forces acting on it are balanced

Explanation: If an object is at rest and stays at rest, the forces acting on it are balanced. This is a consequence of Newton's first law of motion: an object at rest stays at rest unless acted upon by an unbalanced force.

16. Question:

A block and tackle pulley system with 4 ropes lifting the load will have a mechanical advantage of:

A) 1 B) 2 C) 4 D) 8

Answer: C) 4

Explanation: In a block and tackle system, the mechanical advantage is equal to the number of supporting ropes. Therefore, if there are 4 ropes lifting the load, the mechanical advantage is 4.

17. Question:

What is the term used to describe the opposition that a device or material offers to the flow of direct current?

A) Voltage B) Resistance C) Capacitance D) Inductance

Answer: B) Resistance

Explanation: Resistance is the term used to describe the opposition that a device or material offers to the flow of direct current.

18. Question:

Which of the following liquids is most dense at room temperature?

A) Water B) Ethanol C) Mercury D) Gasoline

Answer: C) Mercury

Explanation: Of the options provided, mercury is the densest liquid at room temperature.

19. Question:

Which simple machine is an inclined plane wrapped around a cylinder or cone?

A) Lever B) Wheel and axle C) Pulley D) Screw

Answer: D) Screw

Explanation: A screw is an example of a simple machine that is essentially an inclined plane wrapped around a cylinder or cone.

20. Question:

What happens to a solid object that is denser than the fluid it is placed in?

A) It floats B) It sinks C) It remains stationary D) It dissolves

Answer: B) It sinks

Explanation: If a solid object is denser than the fluid it is placed in, it will sink. This is due to the buoyant force exerted by the fluid, which is less than the weight of the object.

21. Question:

Which of the following states of matter has a definite volume but no definite shape?

A) Solid B) Liquid C) Gas D) Plasma

Answer: B) Liquid

Explanation: Liquids have a definite volume but take the shape of their container. Therefore, they do not have a definite shape.

22. Question:

What type of simple machine is a seesaw?

A) Pulley B) Wheel and axle C) Lever D) Screw

Answer: C) Lever

Explanation: A seesaw is an example of a lever. In a seesaw, the fulcrum (the tilt point) is in the middle, and the forces are applied at the ends.

23. Question:

If you apply a force to an object and it doesn't move, what kind of work are you doing on the object?

A) Positive work B) Negative work C) No work D) Half work

Answer: C) No work

Explanation: In physics, work is defined as the product of the force applied to an object and the distance the object moves in the direction of the force. If the object does not move, no work is done.

24. Question:

What is the unit of measurement for power in the International System of Units?

A) Newton B) Joule C) Watt D) Ampere

Answer: C) Watt

Explanation: Power in the International System of Units is measured in Watts. Power is the rate at which work is done or energy is transferred.

25. Question:

What kind of energy is stored in a stretched rubber band?

A) Kinetic energy B) Potential energy C) Thermal energy D) Electric energy

Answer: B) Potential energy

Explanation: A stretched rubber band has potential energy. When the rubber band is released, the potential energy is converted to kinetic energy as the band snaps back to its resting shape.

26. Question:

Which of these bests describes a scalar quantity?

A) It has both magnitude and direction B) It has only magnitude C) It has only direction D) It has neither magnitude nor direction

Answer: B) It has only magnitude

Explanation: A scalar quantity is defined by its magnitude alone and does not include direction. Examples of scalar quantities include mass, speed, and temperature.

27. Question:

A 1-kilogram mass on Earth will have the same weight on the moon. True or false?

A) True B) False

Answer: B) False

Explanation: The weight of an object is dependent on the gravitational force acting upon it. Because the gravitational force on the moon is about one-sixth of that on Earth, a 1-kilogram mass on Earth will weigh less on the moon.

28. Question:

The force that opposes motion between two surfaces that are in contact is known as:

A) Inertia B) Friction C) Gravity D) Centrifugal

Answer: B) Friction

Explanation: Friction is the force that opposes motion between two surfaces that are in contact with each other.

29. Question:

What does Newton's third law of motion state?

A) An object at rest stays at rest and an object in motion stays in motion B) Force equals mass times acceleration C) For every action, there is an equal and opposite reaction D) The path of an object in motion is always a straight line

Answer: C) For every action, there is an equal and opposite reaction

Explanation: Newton's third law of motion states that for every action, there is an equal and opposite reaction. This means that any force exerted onto a body will create a force of equal magnitude but in the opposite direction on the first object.

30. Question:

A bicycle is an example of which type of machine?

A) Simple machine B) Complex machine C) Compound machine D) Primitive machine

Answer: C) Compound machine

Explanation: A bicycle is an example of a compound machine. It is composed of several simple machines such as wheels and axles (the wheels and pedals), levers (the pedals), and pulleys (the chain and gears).

31. Question:

A screwdriver is used to apply what type of force?

A) Torsional force B) Gravitational force C) Normal force D) Frictional force

Answer: A) Torsional force

Explanation: A screwdriver applies a torsional force, which is a force that causes an object to rotate around an axis.

32. Question:

Which law of motion explains why we need to wear seatbelts in a car?

A) Newton's First Law of Motion B) Newton's Second Law of Motion C) Newton's Third Law of Motion D) Newton's Law of Universal Gravitation

Answer: A) Newton's First Law of Motion

Explanation: Newton's First Law of Motion, also known as the Law of Inertia, states that an object at rest tends to stay at rest and an object in motion tends to stay in motion with the same speed and in the same direction unless acted upon by an unbalanced force. When a car suddenly stops, the passenger tends to keep moving forward. A seatbelt provides the unbalanced force to stop the passenger's motion.

33. Question:

If two gears are meshed together and the first one is turning clockwise, in which direction will the second one turn?

A) Clockwise B) Counterclockwise C) It will not turn D) The direction can't be determined

Answer: B) Counterclockwise

Explanation: In a pair of meshed gears, if one gear is turning in one direction, the other gear will turn in the opposite direction.

34. Question:

What kind of energy does a compressed spring have?

A) Kinetic energy B) Potential energy C) Thermal energy D) Chemical energy

Answer: B) Potential energy

Explanation: A compressed spring has potential energy. This is energy that is stored and can be converted into kinetic energy when the spring is released.

35. Question:

What type of simple machine is a ramp?

A) Lever B) Pulley C) Wheel and axle D) Inclined plane

Answer: D) Inclined plane

Explanation: A ramp is an example of an inclined plane. It allows for less force to be used over a longer distance to move an object upwards.

36. Question:

Which of the following is not a type of friction?

A) Rolling friction B) Sliding friction C) Static friction D) Lateral friction

Answer: D) Lateral friction

Explanation: The three main types of friction are static (between stationary objects), sliding (between objects moving relative to each other), and rolling (involving a rolling object). Lateral friction is not a recognized type of friction.

37. Question:

In terms of energy, what happens when a car is braked to a stop?

A) Kinetic energy is converted into potential energy B) Potential energy is converted into kinetic energy C) Kinetic energy is converted into thermal energy D) Potential energy is converted into thermal energy

Answer: C) Kinetic energy is converted into thermal energy

Explanation: When a car is braked to a stop, the kinetic energy of the car is transformed into thermal energy due to the friction between the brakes and the wheels.

38. Question:

What causes a change in the state of motion of an object?

A) Mass B) Volume C) Inertia D) Force

Answer: D) Force

Explanation: A force causes a change in the state of motion of an object. This is the principle behind Newton's First Law of Motion - an object at rest will stay at rest and an object in motion will stay in motion, unless acted upon by a net external force.

39. Question:

How is energy transferred through a solid?

A) Conduction B) Convection C) Radiation D) Evaporation

Answer: A) Conduction

Explanation: Energy is transferred through a solid by conduction. This process occurs when one particle of an object comes into contact with another and the energy is transferred from one to the other.

40. Question:

What does the buoyant force act on?

A) Only submerged objects B) Only floating objects C) Both submerged and floating objects D) Neither submerged nor floating objects

Answer: C) Both submerged and floating objects

Explanation: The buoyant force, according to Archimedes' principle, acts on both submerged and floating objects. This force equals the weight of the fluid displaced by the object and acts in the upward direction.

41. Question:

Which simple machine consists of an inclined plane wrapped around a cylinder?

A) Lever B) Pulley C) Screw D) Wheel and axle

Answer: C) Screw

Explanation: A screw is a simple machine that consists of an inclined plane wrapped around a cylinder. Turning the screw converts rotational motion into linear motion.

42. Question:

What is the unit of work in the International System of Units (SI)?

A) Joule B) Watt C) Newton D) Pascal

Answer: A) Joule

Explanation: In the International System of Units (SI), the unit of work is the Joule. Work is defined as force times the distance over which it is applied.

43. Question:

Which of the following materials would be the best conductor of electricity?

A) Rubber B) Glass C) Copper D) Wood

Answer: C) Copper

Explanation: Copper is the best conductor of electricity among the materials listed. This is why it is often used in electrical wires and circuits.

44. Question:

How does increasing the surface area affect the pressure exerted by a force?

A) Increases pressure B) Decreases pressure C) Does not affect pressure D) Doubles the pressure

Answer: B) Decreases pressure

Explanation: Increasing the surface area decreases the pressure exerted by a force. Pressure is the ratio of force to the area over which it is distributed. So, for a given force, if the area is increased, the pressure decreases.

45. Question:

What type of energy is stored in an object due to its position?

A) Kinetic energy B) Potential energy C) Mechanical energy D) Thermal energy

Answer: B) Potential energy

Explanation: Potential energy is the energy stored in an object due to its position or configuration. For example, a book on a high shelf has gravitational potential energy because of its position high above the ground.

46. Question:

In a vacuum, which of the following would fall to the ground first?

A) Feather B) Hammer C) Both at the same time D) Neither, they would float

Answer: C) Both at the same time

Explanation: In a vacuum, where there is no air resistance, a feather and a hammer would fall to the ground at the same time. This was famously demonstrated by astronaut David Scott on the moon during the Apollo 15 mission.

47. Question:

What do we call a force that opposes motion between two surfaces that are in contact?

A) Inertia B) Friction C) Gravity D) Centrifugal force

Answer: B) Friction

Explanation: Friction is the force that opposes motion between two surfaces that are in contact. There are several types of friction including static friction (between stationary objects), kinetic friction (between moving objects), and rolling friction (for round objects).

48. Question:

What is the term for a change in the velocity of an object?

A) Momentum B) Acceleration C) Force D) Inertia

Answer: B) Acceleration

Explanation: Acceleration is a change in the velocity of an object. It can be a change in speed, a change in direction, or both.

49. Question:

A wrench is an example of what type of simple machine?

A) Lever B) Wheel and axle C) Pulley D) Screw

Answer: A) Lever

Explanation: A wrench is an example of a lever. When you use a wrench, you apply force at one end to turn a bolt or nut at the other end.

50. Question:

What property of a wave is measured in Hertz?

A) Speed B) Amplitude C) Wavelength D) Frequency

Answer: D) Frequency

Explanation: Frequency, which is the number of wave cycles per second, is measured in Hertz (Hz).

Test Strategies

In the Mechanical Comprehension section of the ASVAB, your understanding of basic mechanical principles and mechanisms will be tested. It might seem intimidating, especially if you don't have much background in physics or mechanics. However, with the right strategies and consistent practice, you can improve your performance on this section of the test. Here are some strategies that might help you do well:

1. Understand Basic Mechanical Principles: The test focuses on basic mechanical and physical principles like force, motion, energy, levers, pulleys, and gears. Make sure you understand these topics. Start by reviewing the basics of physics, paying particular attention to the principles of mechanics.

2. Familiarize Yourself with Common Mechanical Devices: Knowing the common mechanical devices and their functions is important. This includes understanding the functions and principles of operation of devices like screws, gears, pulleys, levers, and incline planes. This knowledge will be valuable in answering the questions that require applied mechanical reasoning.

3. Practice Visualizing: Many of the questions on the test will include diagrams or require you to visualize mechanical scenarios in your mind. Practice visualizing the mechanical concepts you're learning about. For example, if you're learning about how levers work, try to visualize different types of levers and how changing the positions of the fulcrum, effort, and load would affect the operation of the lever.

4. Use Elimination Techniques: If you're unsure of an answer, use elimination techniques to increase your chances of choosing the right one. If you can determine that one or two of the options are definitely wrong, you'll increase your chances of picking the correct answer from the remaining choices.

5. Take Practice Tests: Practice tests are a great way to prepare for the Mechanical Comprehension section. They can help familiarize you with the types of questions you'll encounter and help you understand how to apply your knowledge of mechanical principles. They can also help you identify areas where you need more study.

6. Review Mistakes: When taking practice tests, take the time to review your mistakes. Understanding why you got a question wrong is often as valuable as understanding why you got one right. Use these mistakes as learning opportunities to reinforce your understanding of the material.

7. Manage Your Time: This section of the test is timed, so it's important to manage your time effectively. Don't spend too much time on any one question. If you're stuck, it's often best to make a note, move on, and return to the question if you have time at the end of the test.

Remember, preparation and practice are key. With consistent study and by applying these strategies, you can improve your mechanical comprehension skills and increase your chances of doing well on this portion of the ASVAB.

Chapter 10
Assembling Objects

Overview and Study Guide

The Assembling Objects section of the ASVAB test is designed to measure your spatial perception and ability to understand how different pieces fit together to form a whole. In other words, it evaluates your ability to visualize and think in three dimensions, which is a crucial skill in many military roles.

This test section presents a series of diagrams representing an unassembled object, along with multiple options of how the object might look when assembled. Your task is to choose the option that accurately represents the assembled object. Unlike other sections of the ASVAB, this section does not test your knowledge on a specific subject. Instead, it tests a skill – spatial reasoning.

Here's what you need to know to prepare for this section of the ASVAB:

1. **Understand Spatial Orientation:** Spatial orientation refers to our ability to understand the

positioning of objects in space. It involves being able to visualize how objects look from different angles and how they fit together. Try playing with puzzles or building models to enhance this skill.

2. Practice with Puzzles and Diagrams: One of the best ways to prepare for this section is to practice with puzzles, models, or diagrams that require assembly. This can help develop your ability to visualize how different parts fit together. Jigsaw puzzles, 3D puzzles, and even LEGO sets can be excellent training tools.

3. Understand Different Views: In the Assembling Objects section, you might be asked to identify an object from different views (front, side, top, etc.). Familiarize yourself with these different perspectives and practice visualizing objects from various angles.

4. Develop a Strategy: Some find it helpful to start by looking at the larger pieces in the diagram, and then figuring out where the smaller pieces fit. Others prefer to start with the smaller pieces. Experiment with different strategies and see what works best for you.

5. Practice Under Timed Conditions: The Assembling Objects section is timed, so it's important to practice under similar conditions. Try to complete practice problems within a set timeframe to become more comfortable with the pacing of the test.

Remember, this section of the ASVAB is unique in its focus on spatial reasoning and visualization. The key to success is practice, ideally with puzzles, models, or similar tasks that require you to think spatially and assemble objects mentally. While it might be challenging, it's certainly a skill that can be improved with dedicated preparation and study.

Practice Test with Answers

Note: The "Assembling Objects" section of the ASVAB test is visually based, which means the questions are shown as images or diagrams, rather than written out. For this reason, it's difficult to write out the questions and answers. Typically, you would be shown a disassembled object or a shape, and then you would need to select the correct assembled version from multiple choices.

However, to give you an idea of what these questions might look like, here are some text-based analogues that rely on spatial reasoning:

1. Question:

Consider a cube. Each of its faces is painted red. Now, the cube is cut into 27 smaller, equal-sized cubes. How many of these smaller cubes have only one face painted red?

A) 6 B) 8 C) 12 D) 18

Answer: A) 6

Explanation: The smaller cubes with only one face painted are the cubes in the center of each face of the larger cube. Since a cube has six faces, there are six smaller cubes with only one face painted.

2. Question:

You have a pyramid built with blocks. The top layer has 1 block, the second layer has 4 blocks arranged in a square, the third layer has 9 blocks arranged in a larger square, and so on. If the pyramid has 5 layers, how many blocks are in the pyramid in total?

A) 55 B) 35 C) 50 D) 45

Answer: A) 55

Explanation: The total number of blocks is the sum of the squares of the first five natural numbers. This is because each layer has a square number of blocks

(1^2, 2^2, 3^2, etc.). So, the total is 1^2 + 2^2 + 3^2 + 4^2 + 5^2 = 1 + 4 + 9 + 16 + 25 = 55.

3. Question:

A rectangular box has a width of 2 units, a height of 3 units, and a length of 4 units. If the same amount is added to the width, height, and length of the box, which of the following would result in the greatest increase in the box's volume?

A) Adding 1 unit B) Adding 2 units C) Adding 3 units D) Adding 4 units

Answer: D) Adding 4 units

Explanation: The volume of a rectangular box is calculated as width * height * length. Therefore, adding the same amount to each dimension would result in a larger increase when a larger amount is added.

4. Question:

Which of these shapes has the most sides?

A) Triangle B) Hexagon C) Octagon D) Pentagon

Answer: C) Octagon

Explanation: A triangle has 3 sides, a hexagon has 6, an octagon has 8, and a pentagon has 5. Therefore, the octagon has the most sides.

5. Question:

Consider a regular hexagon (a six-sided figure with all sides of equal length). If you draw all the diagonals from one vertex, how many triangles will you get?

A) 3 B) 4 C) 5 D) 6

Answer: B) 4

Explanation: When you draw all the diagonals from one vertex of a regular hexagon, you divide the hexagon into 4 triangles.

Note: For the actual ASVAB test, you would need to visualize these situations in your mind as you won't be provided with drawn diagrams. It's recommended to practice with actual ASVAB test materials that include visual diagrams to get a feel for the questions.

6. Question:

You have a pyramid built with blocks. The top layer has 1 block, the second layer has 3 blocks arranged in a triangle, the third layer has 6 blocks arranged in a larger triangle, and so on. If the pyramid has 5 layers, how many blocks are in the pyramid in total?

A) 20 B) 25 C) 35 D) 15

Answer: C) 35

Explanation: The total number of blocks is the sum of the first five triangular numbers. This is because each layer forms a triangle with a number of blocks equal to the corresponding triangular number (1, 3, 6, etc.). So, the total is 1 + 3 + 6 + 10 + 15 = 35.

7. Question:

A cylinder and a cone have the same base radius and the same height. If you subtract the volume of the cone from the volume of the cylinder, which of the following will you get?

A) The volume of the cylinder B) The volume of the cone C) Twice the volume of the cone D) Two-thirds the volume of the cylinder

Answer: D) Two-thirds the volume of the cylinder

Explanation: The volume of a cone is one-third the volume of a cylinder with the same base and height. Therefore, subtracting the volume of the cone from the volume of the cylinder leaves two-thirds of the cylinder's volume.

8. Question:

Which of these shapes has more edges?

A) Cube B) Pyramid with a square base C) Tetrahedron (pyramid with a triangular base) D) Octahedron (a figure with 8 faces)

Answer: A) Cube

Explanation: A cube has 12 edges, a pyramid with a square base has 8, a tetrahedron has 6, and an octahedron has 12. Therefore, a cube and an octahedron have the most edges.

9. Question:

If you join all the vertices of a square to a point outside the square, how many triangles are formed?

A) 2 B) 3 C) 4 D) 5

Answer: C) 4

Explanation: By joining all the vertices of a square to a point outside the square, you divide the surrounding space into 4 triangle-shaped regions.

10. Question:

A solid rectangular prism has dimensions 2 cm by 3 cm by 4 cm. All of its edges are painted. The prism is then cut along each edge to form eight smaller, equal-sized rectangular prisms. How many of these smaller prisms have paint on three of their faces?

A) 4 B) 6 C) 8 D) 12

Answer: C) 8

Explanation: The smaller prisms that have paint on three of their faces are the ones at the corners of the original prism. Since a rectangular prism has eight corners, there are eight smaller prisms with three faces painted.

11. Question:

A box contains identical gears that each have 8 teeth. If 12 of these gears are arranged in a line so that each gear meshes with the next one, how many total pairs of teeth come into contact?

A) 48 B) 84 C) 96 D) 108

Answer: C) 96

Explanation: Each gear meshes with its neighbor at two points (one on each side), so each pair of neighboring gears forms two pairs of teeth in contact.

There are 11 pairs of neighbors among 12 gears, so there are 2*11 = 22 pairs of teeth in contact.

12. Question:

Three gears are arranged in a row and mesh together. The first gear has 10 teeth and the second gear has 15 teeth. If the first gear turns 12 times, how many times does the third gear turn, assuming it has 20 teeth?

A) 9 B) 6 C) 3 D) 18

Answer: B) 6

Explanation: The ratio of turns is inversely proportional to the number of teeth. If the first gear turns 12 times, the second gear turns (10/15)*12 = 8 times. The third gear then turns (15/20)*8 = 6 times.

13. Question:

In a certain gear assembly, Gear A with 20 teeth is directly meshed with Gear B with 30 teeth. If Gear A makes 10 rotations, how many rotations will Gear B make?

A) 15 B) 20 C) 30 D) 10

Answer: A) 15

Explanation: The number of rotations of meshed gears is inversely proportional to the number of teeth. Therefore, if Gear A makes 10 rotations, Gear B will make $(20/30)10 = 15/310 = 15$ rotations.

14. Question:

A cube is painted blue on all faces, then cut into 27 smaller cubes. How many of the smaller cubes have exactly two faces painted?

A) 6 B) 12 C) 18 D) 24

Answer: B) 12

Explanation: Only the smaller cubes that lie in the center of each edge of the original cube have exactly two faces painted. Since a cube has 12 edges, there are 12 such smaller cubes.

15. Question:

What is the total surface area (in square units) of a cube whose edge is 5 units?

A) 25 B) 50 C) 100 D) 150

Answer: D) 150

Explanation: A cube has 6 faces, and the area of each face of this cube is 5^5 = 25 square units. Therefore, the total surface area is 6·25 = 150 square units.

16. Question:

In a puzzle, you have to assemble six square pieces each with side length of 2 cm into a larger square. What is the side length of the assembled square?

A) 2 cm B) 4 cm C) 6 cm D) 8 cm

Answer: B) 4 cm

Explanation: Since you're arranging 6 squares into a larger square, the total area of the large square is 6·2² = 24 square cm. The side length of a square with this area is the square root of 24, which is between 4 and 5. Since the side length of the large square must be an integer multiple of the side length of the small squares, the only possible side length is 4 cm.

17. Question:

An octahedron (a solid figure with eight faces) has how many edges?

A) 8 B) 10 C) 12 D) 14

Answer: C) 12

Explanation: An octahedron has 8 faces, 12 edges, and 6 vertices. You can remember this by noting that an octahedron is a dual polyhedron to a cube, which has 6 faces, 12 edges, and 8 vertices.

18. Question:

A cube has a volume of 64 cubic cm. What is the length of one edge?

A) 2 cm B) 3 cm C) 4 cm D) 6 cm

Answer: C) 4 cm

Explanation: The volume of a cube is the cube of the edge length. So, if the volume is 64 cubic cm, the edge length is the cube root of 64, which is 4 cm.

19. Question:

Which solid figure has one surface that is a circle and one surface that is a point?

A) Cylinder B) Sphere C) Cone D) Cube

Answer: C) Cone

Explanation: A cone has a base that is a circle and a vertex (point) at the top where all the side surfaces meet.

20. Question:

A cylindrical can has a radius of 3 cm and a height of 10 cm. What is its volume?

A) 30 cubic cm B) 90 cubic cm C) 270 cubic cm D) 283.5 cubic cm

Answer: D) 283.5 cubic cm

Explanation: The volume of a cylinder is given by the formula $V = \pi r^2 h$, where r is the radius and h is the height. Therefore, the volume of this can is $V = \pi*(3 \text{ cm})^2*(10 \text{ cm}) = 283.5$ cubic cm.

Test Strategies

The Assembling Objects (AO) subtest of the ASVAB is often considered one of the more challenging sections. It tests your spatial visualization ability and understanding of how different parts fit together to form a whole. This is a critical skill in many technical and engineering roles in the Navy.

Here are some strategies to help you perform well in this section:

1. **Understand the Basics of Spatial Reasoning:** Get comfortable with 3D shapes and their 2D representations. Practice visualizing objects from different angles and perspectives. You can use

physical objects around you or use online resources for 3D shape manipulation exercises.

2. **Familiarize Yourself with Common Shapes and Structures:** In the AO section, you'll often see common shapes like cubes, cylinders, and pyramids. Understand how these shapes look from different perspectives and how they fit together.

3. **Practice with Puzzles:** Puzzles like jigsaw puzzles, 3D puzzles, and Rubik's cubes can be very useful for developing your spatial reasoning and assembly skills.

4. **Use the Process of Elimination:** Often, you can eliminate some answer choices just by looking at them. If a piece in an answer choice obviously doesn't fit, or if the assembled object doesn't match the target shape, eliminate that choice.

5. **Use a Step-by-Step Approach:** Start with the largest or most obvious pieces first and see how smaller pieces fit around them. This can often make the process easier.

6. **Don't Rush:** Although the ASVAB is a timed test, don't rush through the questions. Mistakes often

happen when candidates feel rushed. Take the time to carefully consider each question.

7. **Stay Calm:** If a question seems too complicated, don't panic. Take a few deep breaths, eliminate the obvious wrong answers, and concentrate on the remaining options. Remember that sometimes the answer is simpler than it initially seems.

In the end, the key to success on the Assembling Objects subtest, like all sections of the ASVAB, is practice. The more you familiarize yourself with these types of questions and the more you exercise your spatial reasoning abilities, the better you will likely perform. Keep practicing and you'll improve your skills and confidence over time.

Chapter 11

Exam Day Tips and Strategies

Preparing for the Test Day

The night before and the morning of your test can play a pivotal role in your performance. Here are some tips and strategies to ensure you're in the best possible shape, mentally and physically, when you start your test:

1. **Rest Well**: Get a good night's sleep the night before the test. Your mind needs time to recharge and relax. If you go into the test feeling exhausted, it can significantly affect your concentration and performance.

2. **Eat a Balanced Meal**: Your brain needs fuel to work effectively. Have a healthy, balanced meal before your test. Include protein, healthy fats, and slow-releasing carbohydrates to keep your energy levels stable.

3. **Hydrate**: Stay hydrated, but don't drink excessive amounts of water right before or during the test to avoid frequent bathroom breaks.

4. **Review, Don't Cram**: Look over your study materials the night before, but avoid the temptation to cram. This late in the game, you're unlikely to learn new material, and the stress can impair your performance on test day.

5. **Pack the Night Before**: Gather everything you need for the test (ID, watch, extra pencils, etc.) the night before. This way, you avoid last-minute rushing and stress in the morning.

6. **Dress Comfortably**: Dress in layers so you can adjust based on the room temperature. Comfortable clothing will allow you to focus on the test rather than your discomfort.

7. **Arrive Early**: Plan to arrive at least 15 minutes early. This gives you time to get comfortable in your surroundings and avoid unnecessary stress caused by running late.

8. **Mindset Matters**: Maintain a positive mindset. Remember that it's normal to feel nervous before

a test. Take deep breaths and reassure yourself that you've prepared as well as you can.

9. **Read Instructions Carefully**: Once the test starts, make sure to read all instructions and questions carefully. Don't rush. It's better to spend a few extra seconds understanding the question than to lose points over a misunderstanding.

10. **Pace Yourself**: Keep track of the time, but don't let it make you anxious. If you don't know an answer, don't spend too much time on it. Mark it, move on, and if time allows, come back to it at the end.

Remember, the ASVAB is not a measure of your worth—it's simply a tool to assess your understanding of various subjects. Do your best, stay positive, and know that preparation is the key to success.

Strategies for During the Test

Once you're seated and the test begins, it's crucial to keep some strategies in mind to help you navigate through the test questions most effectively. These strategies will help you optimize your time and increase your chances of a higher score:

1. **Time Management**: Every section in the ASVAB is timed. It's essential to be mindful of the clock, but don't let it overwhelm you. Try to pace yourself so you can answer as many questions as possible within the allotted time. It's a good idea to quickly move through questions you find easy and spend more time on those you find challenging.

2. **Read Each Question Carefully**: Misreading a question can lead to incorrect answers even if you know the right solution. Make sure you understand what's being asked before you start working on your answer.

3. **Process of Elimination**: If you're unsure about a question, try to eliminate incorrect answers first. This process increases your chances of choosing the right answer if you have to guess.

4. **Skip and Return**: If a question seems too complicated or time-consuming, don't be afraid to skip it and return to it later. It's better to answer all the questions you're sure about first, then use

any remaining time to work on the more challenging ones.

5. **Educated Guessing**: There's no penalty for wrong answers on the ASVAB, so make sure you answer every question, even if you're not sure of the right answer. An educated guess is better than no answer at all.

6. **Watch for Traps**: The ASVAB test makers sometimes include "distractor" answers that may seem right but aren't. Be mindful of these, and don't rush to select an answer because it seems immediately apparent.

7. **Use the Test Paper**: If scratch paper is provided during the test, use it to your advantage. Jot down quick notes, solve problems, or mark questions you want to revisit if time allows.

8. **Trust Your First Instinct**: Studies show that your first answer choice is often correct. Unless you have a strong reason to change your answer, it's usually best to trust your initial instinct.

9. **Stay Calm**: Test anxiety can negatively impact your performance. If you start feeling

overwhelmed, take a moment to close your eyes, take a deep breath, and regain your composure.

Remember, the goal of the ASVAB isn't just to assess what you already know—it's also designed to measure your potential to learn and adapt. So, keep a positive attitude, do your best, and let your preparation guide you.

What to Do After the Test

Completing the ASVAB is a significant accomplishment, and after hours of study and preparation, it can feel like a substantial weight lifted off your shoulders. But what comes next? Here are some guidelines on what to do after the test:

1. **Relax and Reflect**: Immediately after the test, give yourself a moment to relax. It's essential to let your mind unwind and reward yourself for your hard work. Then, while the test is still fresh in your mind, reflect on your performance. Try to identify the areas where you felt confident and those where you struggled. This reflection is especially useful if you plan to retake the test in the future.

2. **Review Your Scores**: Once your scores are available, take time to review them thoroughly. The ASVAB provides scores for individual areas as well as a cumulative score. Review each section to see where your strengths and weaknesses lie.

3. **Understand the Results**: ASVAB scores are used to determine qualifications for various military occupations and enlistment bonuses. Understanding your scores is crucial to knowing what opportunities are available to you. If you have any doubts or need clarification, don't hesitate to ask a military recruiter or a guidance counselor.

4. **Reevaluate and Plan**: If your scores don't meet the expectations or requirements for your desired role, it might be necessary to retake the test. Review your reflection on the areas you struggled with and devise a study plan that focuses on improving in those areas.

5. **Consider Professional Advice**: If you're still unsure about interpreting your scores or the next steps, consider seeking advice from a career counselor. They can provide you with information

on various military occupations that align with your scores and career aspirations.

6. **Keep Your Options Open**: Remember that the ASVAB is just one measure of your abilities and potential. While it's an important part of your military career, it doesn't define you. Consider exploring other options within the military that may be a good fit, and be open to discovering new paths.

Remember, taking the ASVAB is a step toward your future in the military. Whether your scores are high or lower than expected, it's a learning experience that can help guide you to the right career path in the military. Keep your head up, and don't be afraid to pursue your goals!

Chapter 12

Conclusion

As we come to the end of this comprehensive guide to the ASVAB Navy Practice Test, we hope that you feel more confident and prepared to tackle the exam. This book has been designed as a tool to support your learning journey, providing valuable insights, strategies, and practice materials to aid your success.

The ASVAB exam, a vital part of the recruitment process for the U.S. Navy, is a multifaceted test that assesses your capabilities across a range of subjects. From General Science to Mechanical Comprehension, each section of the ASVAB requires its unique set of skills and knowledge. Preparing for this diverse exam can feel daunting, but remember that every effort you make brings you one step closer to your goal.

Over the course of this guide, we have delved into each section of the ASVAB, discussing its importance, providing study guides, and giving you the chance to practice with unique questions. Furthermore, we've provided test strategies specific to each section, equipping you with techniques to manage your time effectively, tackle tricky questions, and maintain your composure under exam conditions.

Chapter 11 offered tips and strategies for the test day, providing guidance on how to prepare beforehand, what strategies to use during the test, and how to review your performance afterward. While the test day can feel stressful, remember that adequate preparation, relaxation, and reflection are key to a successful experience.

Finally, remember that while the ASVAB is important, it does not define your worth or potential. It is merely a tool used to help identify where your strengths lie within the vast field of military occupations. Whatever your score, there is a place for you in the U.S. Navy that will allow you to serve your country with pride and honor.

So, keep your head high and your spirits higher as you take this next step in your military career. Whether you're about to take the test for the first time or you're revisiting for a higher score, we wish you every success. Go forth with confidence and give it your best shot! You have the tools, the knowledge, and the determination to succeed. Good luck!

Key Takeaways

As we wrap up this comprehensive guide to the ASVAB Navy Practice Test, it's time to reflect on the key takeaways from each chapter. This journey has provided a wealth of information designed to guide your preparations and increase your confidence as you approach the test. Here are the essential points we hope you'll carry forward.

1. **The Importance of ASVAB for Navy Recruits**: Remember that the ASVAB is not just a test; it is a doorway to your future in the U.S. Navy. Your score determines not just your eligibility, but also the range of career paths available to you. Therefore, preparation is key.

2. **Content Knowledge Across Various Fields**: From General Science to Assembling Objects, the ASVAB covers a range of subjects. Each chapter's study guide offered an overview and detailed explanations of core topics, ensuring a comprehensive understanding.

3. **Practice, Practice, Practice**: Throughout the book, practice tests specific to each section have been provided. These give you hands-on

experience with the style of questions you will encounter in the actual test, thus enhancing your problem-solving speed and accuracy.

4. **Test-Taking Strategies**: Each chapter provided unique strategies to tackle its respective section. From time management techniques to handling difficult questions, these strategies are designed to help you approach the test confidently and calmly.

5. **Simulated Exam Experience**: The full-length practice tests have been crafted to mirror the actual ASVAB, thus providing a realistic experience of the exam day. Use these tests to evaluate your readiness and identify areas needing further focus.

6. **Preparation Beyond Studies**: Chapter 11 highlighted that preparation goes beyond academic readiness. Physical health, mental well-being, and proper rest are equally important. Moreover, it provided guidance on what to do during and after the test.

7. **Perseverance and Resilience**: Lastly, always remember that the path to success is paved with perseverance. Stay dedicated to your studies, but

also be patient with yourself. Every mistake is an opportunity to learn and grow.

Remember, the journey to joining the U.S. Navy is a marathon, not a sprint. Use this guide as your roadmap, and remember that consistent effort, strategic planning, and a positive mindset are your best allies on this journey. As you close this book and move on to the next chapter of your ASVAB journey, we wish you the best of luck. May you find success and fulfill your dreams of serving in the U.S. Navy

Further Study Recommendations

Now that we have explored the entirety of the ASVAB Navy Practice Test, provided you with a multitude of practice questions, and discussed various test-taking strategies, it's crucial to talk about recommendations for further study. Despite the comprehensive nature of this guide, continuous learning and improvement are key to excelling at the ASVAB.

1. **Diversify Your Study Resources**: While this book offers an extensive overview and numerous practice questions, it's beneficial to diversify your resources. Seek out additional textbooks, find

relevant websites, use educational apps, and join online study groups. Remember, a variety of perspectives can deepen your understanding and improve your ability to answer a broader range of questions.

2. **Take Full-Length Practice Exams Regularly**: The full-length practice tests in this guide are a great resource, but don't stop here. Regularly taking practice tests under exam-like conditions can enhance your endurance, speed, and ability to handle pressure.

3. **Review Wrong Answers**: When you get a question wrong on a practice test, take the time to understand why. Go back to the relevant section in this guide or your other resources, review the material, and ensure you understand your mistake. This active learning process will prevent you from repeating the same mistake on the real test.

4. **Focus on Your Weak Areas**: While it's important to maintain your strengths, focusing on your weak areas can lead to significant score improvements. Don't shy away from the hard stuff—embrace it.

5. **Enroll in Prep Courses**: If you're finding self-study challenging, consider enrolling in a prep course for the ASVAB. A structured course with an experienced instructor can provide personalized guidance and feedback, enhancing your study efficiency.

6. **Stay Updated**: The ASVAB, like any standardized test, can undergo changes in format or content emphasis. Keep an eye on the official ASVAB website for any updates or modifications to the test.

7. **Mind and Body Wellness**: Remember to balance your rigorous study regime with proper rest, nutrition, and exercise. A healthy mind and body contribute significantly to your performance on test day.

Remember, the aim of the ASVAB is not just to test your knowledge, but also to evaluate your potential to train for various Navy jobs. Therefore, your persistence, resilience, and willingness to continuously learn and improve are as valuable as the knowledge you've gained from this guide.

Continue your journey with these further study recommendations, and may each step you take bring you closer to your goal of serving in the U.S. Navy.

www.ingramcontent.com/pod-product-compliance
Ingram Content Group UK Ltd.
Pitfield, Milton Keynes, MK11 3LW, UK
UKHW041305180426
11947UKWH00009B/687